PILIPINO-ENGLISH/ ENGLISH-PILIPINO PHRASEBOOK AND DICTIONARY

RAYMOND P. BARRAGER

JESUSA V. SALVADOR

HIPPOCRENE BOOKS
New York

For information, contact:
HIPPOCRENE BOOKS, INC.
171 Madison Avenue
New York, NY 10016

Library of Congress Cataloging-in-Publication Data

Barrager, Raymond P.
        Pilipino-Englilsh, English-Pilipino phrasebook and dictionary /
    Raymond P. Barrager, Jesusa V. Salvador.
            p.   cm.   -- (Hippocrene concise dictionary)
            ISBN 0-7818-0451-5
            1. Tagalog language--Conversation and phrase books--English.
    2. Tagalog language--Dictionaries--English. 3. English language-
    -Dictionaries--Tagalog. I. Salvador, Jesusa V. II. Title.
    III. Series.
    PL6055.B37   1996
    499'.21183421--dc20   95-50676
                                                              CIP

CONTENTS

25 IMPORTANT WORDS AND PHRASES

1. Good Morning.............. **Magandáng umága**
2. Good Afternoon........... **Magandáng hápon**
3. Good Evening/Night....... **Magandáng gábi**
4. How are you?.............. **Kumustá ka (kayó)?**
5. I'm fine...................... **Mabúti akó.**
6. Thank you................... **Salámat**
7. You're welcome........... **Waláng anumán.**
8. Do you know English?.... **Marúnong ba kayó nang Ingles?**
9. What is your name?....... **Anóng pangálan mo?**
10. It is nice to meet you.... **Ikinagagalak kong mákilala kayó.**
11. Excuse me (I'm sorry)... **Patáwad pô.**
12. No more (thank you)..... **Huwág na (salámat).**
13. How much?................. **Magkáno?**
14. Yes/No...................... **Oó/Hindî**
15. Left/Right.................. **Kaliwâ/Kánan**
16. Here/There................ **Dito/Doon**
17. Man/Woman.............. **Laláki/Babáe**
18. Restroom................... **"Comfort Room" (CR)**
19. Where is the toilet?....... **Nasaán ang kasílyas?**
20. Who is there?.............. **Sino iyán?**
21. Come in..................... **Tulóy**
22. I do not understand....... **Hindî ko naintindihán.**
23. I do not speak Tagalog.. **Hindî akó marúnong nang Tagálog.**
24. So long...................... **O, síge na**
25. OK........................... **Síge**

INTRODUCTION

The purpose of this phrasebook is to acquaint visitors, or indeed anyone with little to no knowledge of Pilipino, with some of the more common words and phrases of the language. Also included is a brief description of Pilipino grammar, enabling the reader to expand on the phrases given by substituting nouns, pronouns, adjectives, etc. Pilipino grammar is a very difficult subject and a full description is beyond the scope of this book. However, it is hoped that the brief description provided will be a useful guide to the reader who wishes to use the phrases given with confidence and accuracy. The aim is to provide a basis for simple conversation, to encourage the reader to proceed further on his or her own account, and acquire a working knowledge of Pilipino.

The best way to learn a language is to hear it spoken in its natural environment and this book may provide an incentive to do just that. Anyone interested in taking the subject a step further will find that only a few Pilipino dictionaries and language texts are available outside of the Philippines. One will find, however, that the native Pilipino speaker is the best source of assistance. Though not a necessity to know the local language, as about half of the population has a basic knowledge of English, the locals will be both pleased and surprised if you are able to speak even a few words.

No visit to the Philippines can be as rewarding as one where the visitor has experienced first-hand the warm hospitality of one of Asia's most enchanting countries. The ability to speak just a few words and phrases may be the key to unlocking the doors to the Philippines.

ABOUT THE PILIPINO LANGUAGE

In reality, as yet, there is no such thing as a true national Pilipino language. Some 70 plus languages are spoken throughout the islands. Eight languages, all belonging to the Malayo-Polynesian language family and hence related to Indonesian and Malay, are spoken by about 90 percent of the population. Of these primary eight languages - Tagalog, Cebuano, Illocano, Hiligaynon, Bikol, Waray-Waray, Pampango, and Pangasinan - no two are mutually comprehensible and each have a number of dialects. Speakers of Visayan Islands languages - Cebuano, Waray-Waray, and Ilongo - find communication with each other easier than with Tagalogs or Illocanos.

The concept of a national language emerged during the Spanish colonial period. Spanish was introduced by the colonial masters and taught in the schools. Since education was a prerogative of the wealthy, Spanish developed as the language of business and politics, while the masses continued speaking their regional languages. The concept of a national (Pilipino) language emerged after the 1896 Spanish-American War but remained dormant until 1936, the year in which the National Language Institute was established. In that year, one year after the formation of the Philippine Commonwealth, President Manuel Quezon declared Tagalog as the national language of the Philippines.

Tagalog, as the most developed and widely understood of the Philippine languages, is spoken by well over 10 million people. It is the language of the capital city and the eight provinces surrounding Manila as well as a number of islands and areas far from the capital. Thus, Tagalog, with linguistic elements from other Philippine languages was confirmed and incorporated into the Philippine Constitution in 1946 as the national Pilipino language.

During the American colonial period, English emerged as an official language. Since total independence from the United States in 1946, English has remained the language of commerce, government, and international relations. In 1974, a policy of bilingualism was initiated to gradually phase English out of schools, business, and government while fostering the use of Pilipino in its place. At government insistence the use of Pilipino has spread throughout both the nation and the media. Pilipino has been taught in schools and universities since 1978. However, Filipinos have refused to accept one national language at the expense of their regional languages. Language divisions among Filipinos are important and the government policy of promoting Pilipino has come under attack. English has remained the language of commerce and politics but increasingly Pilipino serves as the common language.

BASIC GRAMMAR

Since Pilipino grammar or syntax is not constructed along English (or Spanish) lines, a basic explanation of Pilipino grammar is provided to familiarize the reader with the rather complex nature of Pilipino. You will find grammar notes throughout the sections to facilitate your comprehension of the Pilipino language.

Grammar Notes: *In Pilipino, the verb does not change whether the subject is singular or plural.*

Verbs

The Pilipino verb form is the most difficult part of the language to learn. The basis for the verb is the "root". Not counting the imperative (commands) there are five classes of verbs: **indicative** (mag-, -um, ma-, i-, -in, -an & pag-an verbs), **distributive** (mang- & pang--in verbs), **aptative** (maka- and ma verbs), **social** (maki- & paki- verbs), **causative** (magpa-, pa--in, pa--an, & ipa- verbs). There are five foci of a verb: Actor Focus, Goal Focus, Locative Focus, Benefactive Focus, and Instrumental Focus.

The Pilipino verb system does not have the same tense distinctions as English.

There are four <u>aspects</u> (so called "tenses") of a Pilipino verb:

Neutral: (the infinitive)

Completed: (for action started
                       and terminated - **past**)

Incomplete: (for action started but not
                       completed - **present**)

Contemplated: (for action not started -
                       future)

Typical Conjugation Patterns (Actor Focus)

For **UM** prefixed Verbs

<u>With root beginning with a vowel</u>

Root:	**alis**	(to leave)
Infinitive:	**umalis** (prefix + root)	(to leave)
Completed:	**umalis** (prefix + root)	(left)
Incomplete:	**umaalis** (prefix+1st syllable reduplicated+root)	(leaving)
Contemplated:	**aalis** (1st syllable of root reduplicated+ root)	(will leave)

<u>With root beginning with a consonant</u>

Root	**kain**	(to eat)
Infinitive:	**kumain** (prefix inserted after 1st consonant)	(to eat)
Completed:	**kumain** (prefix inserted after 1st consonant)	(ate)
Incomplete:	**kumakain** (prefix inserted and 1st syllable repeated)	(eating)
Contemplated:	**kakain** (1st syllable repeated + root)	(will eat)

For MAG- prefixed verbs

With root beginning with a vowel

Root: **aral** (to study)

Infinitive: **mag-aral** (to study)
(prefix+hyphen+root)

Completed: **nag-aral** (studied)
(change *mag* to *nag*)

Incomplete: **nag-aaral** (studying)
(*nag*+hyphen+repeated 1st syllable+root)

Contemplated: **mag-aaral** (will study)
(*mag*+hyphen+repeated 1st syllable+root)

With root beginning with a consonant

Root: **luto** (to cook)

Infinitive: **magluto** (to cook) (prefix+root)

Completed: **nagluto** (cooked)
(change *mag* to *nag*)

Incomplete: **nagluluto** (cooking)
(*nag*+repeated 1st syllable+root)

Contemplated: **magluluto** (will cook)
(*mag*+repeated 1st syllable+root)

Similar conjugation patterns exist for each of the other four foci. Thus the root "**alis**" (to leave) has approximately 20 variations in its **um-** prefixed form. A root such as "**putol**" (to cut something) which can be used to form **um-**, **mag-**, **mang-**, **maka-**, **makapag-**, **maki-**, and **magpa-** prefixed verbs has approximately 140 variations.

SENTENCE STRUCTURE

There are two sentence structures in Pilipino:

1) The natural order sentence:
   (The subject comes before the predicate)

> **"Ang kama ay maliit."**
> "The bed is small."

2) The transposed order sentence:
   (The predicate comes before the subject)

> **"Maliit ang kama."**
> "Small is the bed."

Filipinos tend to utilize the transposed order, especially in oral communications.

STRESSES & ACCENTS

Stresses are vocal emphasis on a particular syllable *(There are four stresses in Pilipino).*

Accents are symbols placed over a vowel to indicate the type of stress.

a. **Acute Stress**: Vocal emphasis placed on a particular syllable. The **acute ' accent** is used to mark this stress.

Examples:

*an**Á**K*   child   *in**Á***   mother

b. **Penultimate Stress**: Vocal emphasis on the syllable before the last. The **acute accent** also marks this stress.

Examples:

laL**Á**ki   man   baB**Á**e   woman

c. **Penultimate Stress and glottal catch**: A slightly heavy vocal stress is given to the next to last syllable. The vowel at the end of the word is cut short or stopped. A **grave accent `** is placed above the last vowel in the word to mark this stress.

Examples:

SUsì   key   *PUnò*   tree

d. **Acute Glottal**: Stress is placed on the last syllable and the vowel at the end of the word is cut short. The accent is the **circumflex ^**. It is placed above the last vowel.

Examples:

*ginT**Ô***   gold   *puN**Ô***   full

Stress placement can change the meaning of words (notice *punò* and *punô* in the previous examples).

When a word is long it may have one or two stressed syllables.

In normal written materials, accent marks are not indicated. One must learn where proper accents are required. Accents are shown in the phrasebook to facilitate the beginner's pronunciation.

In conversation, glottal vowels cease to be pronounced with a catch except when they appear as phrase or sentence ends.

The sound of *"o"* in syllable ending words is changed to *"u"* to facilitate pronunciation.

PRONUNCIATION

Pilipino words are pronounced exactly as they are spelled.

Vowels are pronounced separately and distinctly.

Pilipino and Spanish vowels are pronounced identically.

Pilipino and Spanish consonants are pronounced similarly.

THE ALPHABET

Composed of only twenty letters, five vowels
and 15 consonants.

A (ah); **B** (beh); **K** (kah); **D** (deh); **E** (eh); **G**
(heh); **H** (ah-cheh); **I** (ee); **L** (el-leh); **M** (em-
meh); **N** (en-eh); **Ng** (en-nee-heh); **O** (oh); **P**
(peh); **R** (er-reh); **S** (es-seh); **T** (teh); **U** (oo); **W**
(doh bleh-oo); **Y** (ee'gree'aygah)

Vowels

A	ah	as in "<u>a</u>lms"
E	eh	as in "<u>e</u>nd"
I	ee	as in "<u>e</u>vening"
O	oh	as in "<u>o</u>bey"
U	oo	as in "f<u>oo</u>d"

Consonants (pronounced with the sound of
"a" after the consonant)

B	Ba	**K**	Ka
D	Da	**G**	Ga
H	Ha	**L**	La
M	Ma	**N**	Na
NG	NGa	**P**	Pa
R	Ra	**S**	Sa
T	Ta	**W**	Wa
		Y	Ya

English and Spanish letters not found in the Philipino alphabet are:

C CH F J LL Ñ Q RR V X Z

Previously these letters were only used in names of persons, places, and, in rare instances, in some foreign words borrowed into the Pilipino language. When used they are pronounced as follows:

C (*theh*)	**LL** (*el'lee-eh*)	**RR** (*er'rreh*)
CH (*cheh*)	**Ñ** (*en'nee- heh*)	**V** (*veh*)
F (*ef'feh*)	**Q** (*koo*)	**X** (*eh'kees*)
J (*hoh'tah*)		**Z** (*zeh-tah*)

To incorporate sounds of these letters:
Hard **C** is changed to **K**   **F** is changed to **P**
J is changed to **H**   Soft **C** is changed to **S**
LL is changed to **LY**   **Q** is changed to **K**
CH is changed to **TS**   **V** is changed to **B**
X is changed to **KS**   **Z** is changed to **S**
a written **W** is often pronounced as **U**
F, **P** and **Ph** are interchangeable, so are **B** and **V**.

Due to the fact that the modern Pilipino alphabet is a borrowed alphabet, many non-Pilipino letters began appearing in the language. So common was this practice that these letters are now being taught in schools. It is very common to see a foreign word spelled in its original language as well as in Pilipino (e.g. **taxi** or **taksi**).

Foreign words (mainly Spanish and English) are common in Pilipino. Technically, when spelled in their original language, they remain "foreign" but when changed to conform with the Pilipino alphabet they become Pilipino. The names of persons and places are not changed.

From English

football	**putbol**
boxing	**boksing**
manager	**manedyer**
janitor	**dyanitor**

From Spanish

calle	**calye**
lapiz	**lapis**
telefono	**telepono**
silla	**silya**

To facilitate your pronounciation, divide words into syllables as: **magandá** (beautiful) = ma-gan-dá (pronounced: mah gahn DAH).
If you have difficulty dividing Pilipino words into syllables, familiarize yourself with the four "syllable types" shown below:

1. The **Simple** consisting of one vowel (V):

as the:	"*o*"	in	"ta-*o*"	*(person)*
as the:	"*a*"	in	"pa-*a*"	*(foot)*
as the:	"*u*"	in	"*u*-lo"	*(head)*
as the:	"*i*" or "*a*"	in	"*i*-*a*-lis"	*(to be removed)*

2. The **Consonant-Vowel** syllable (CV):

as the:	"*ta*"	in	"*ta*-o"	(*person*)
as the:	"*pa*"	in	"*pa*-a"	(*foot*)
as the:	"*lo*"	in	"u-*lo*"	(*head*)
as the:	"*ba*"or "*sa*"	in	"*ba*-*sa*"	(*read*)

3. The Vowel-Consonant syllable (VC):

as the:	"*an*"	in	"*an*-tay"	(*wait*)
as the:	"*ak*"	in	"*ak*-yat"	(*climb*)
as the:	"*it* "	in	"mali-*it* "	(*small*)
as the	"*an*" or "*ak*"	in	"*an*-*ak*"	(*child*)

4. The Consonant-Vowel-Consonant (CVC):

as the:	"*tay*"	in	"an-*tay*"	(*wait*)
as the:	"*yat*"	in	"ak-*yat*"	(*climb*)
as the:	"*law*"	in	"i-*law*"	(*light*)
as the:	"*lis*"	in	"i-a-*lis*"	(*to be removed*)

Three very common Philipino words tend to confuse most English speakers. These words are **ng**, **nga**, & **mga**.

ng is pronounced "*nahng*" and for our elementary purposes means "**of**".

nga is pronounced "*ngah*" and means "**really**" or "**please**" in requests.

mga is pronounced "*mahng-AH*"and denotes plurality in count nouns.
(e.g. **aso** = dog; <u>mga</u> aso = dogs
baro = dress; <u>mga</u> baro = dresses)

CARDINAL NUMBERS

Cultural Notes: *If you know Spanish you have an advantage. Spanish numbers are commonly used throughout the Philippines.*

#	Spanish Set	Pilipino Set
0	séro	walâ
1	úno	isá
2	dós	dalawá
3	trés	tatló
4	kuwárto	ápat
5	síngko	limá
6	séis	ánim
7	siyéte	píto
8	ótso	waló
9	nuwébe	siyám
10	diyés	sampû
11	ónse	labíng-isá
12	dóse	labíngdalawá
13	tríse	labíntatló
14	katórse	labíng-ápat
15	kínse	labínlimá
16	disiseís	labing-ánim
17	disisyéte	labimpito
18	disiótso	labingwalo
19	disinuwébe	labinsiyám
20	béyente	dalawampû
21	béynte úno	dalawampú't isá
30	tréynta	tatlumpû
32	tréynta'y dos	tatlumpú't dalawá
40	kuwarénta	apatnapû
43	kuwarénta'y trés	apatnapút tatló
50	singkuwénta	limampû

56	sinkuwénta'y séis	limampú't aním
60	sesénta	animnapû
65	sesénta'y síngko	animnapú't limá
70	seténta	pitumpû
74	seténta'y kuwárto	pitumpú't ápat
80	otsénta	walumpû
87	otsénta'y siyéte	walumpú't pitó
90	nobénta	siyamnapû
98	nobénta'y ótso	siyamnapú't waló
100	siyénto	isáng daán; sandaán
101	siyénto úno	isáng daá't isá
105	siyénto síngko	isáng daá't limá
109	siyénto nuwébe	isáng daá't siyám
200	dós siyéntos	dalawáng daán
203	dós siyéntos trés	dalawáng daán at tatló
300	trés siyéntos	tatlóng daán
400	kuwátro siyéntos	ápat na raán
500	kinyéntos	limáng daán
600	séis siyéntos	ánim na raán
608	séis siyéntos ótso	ánim na raán at waló
700	siyéte siyéntos	pitóng daán
800	ótso siyéntos	walóng daán
900	nuwébe siyentos	siyám na raán
1000	mil	isáng líbo
5000	singko mil	limáng líbo
10000	diyés mil	isáng laksá
100,000	siyento mil	isáng yúta
1,000,000	milyón	isáng ángaw; isáng milyón
1,000,000,000	bilyón	isáng líbong ángaw; isáng bilyón

ORDINAL NUMBERS

Pilipino has three sets of ordinal numbers.

Two ordinal number sets are Tagalog based. One set is prefixed by **ika-** (beginning with 2nd) and is the most common of the Tagalog based sets. One set is prefixed by **pang-** and is seldom used.

	IKA-	PANG-
1st	úna	panguná
2nd	ikalawá	pangalawá
3rd	ikatló	pangatló
4th	ika-ápat	pang-ápat
5th	ika-limá	pang-limá
6th	ika-ánim	pang-ánim
7th	ika-pitó	pang-pitó
8th	ika-waló	pang-waló
9th	ika-siyám	pang-siyám
10th	ika-sampû	pang-sampû
11th	ika-labíng-isá	pang-labíng-isá
20th	ika-dalawampû	pang-dalawampû
30th	ika-tatlumpû	pang-tatlumpû
40th	ika-apatnapû	pang-apatnapû
50th	ika-limampû	pang-limampû
100th	ikasandaán	pangsandaán

The third ordinal number set is Spanish based and used more often than its "ika" - prefixed counterpart. This set prefixes an "**A**" to a Spanish number to **express dates** and **days of the month.**

1st.......	**a-priméro**	10th.....	**a-diyés**
2rd.......	**a-dós**	11th.....	**a-ónse**
3rd.......	**a-trés**	12th.....	**a-dóse**
4th.......	**a-kuwátro**	15th.....	**a-kínse**
5th.......	**a-sínko**	20th.....	**a-béynte**

MORE ABOUT NUMBERS

To add "**each**" to a number (e.g. "**one each**")
add "**tig-**" before the number.

one each............	**tig-isá**
two each............	**tigalawá***
three each..........	**tigatló***
four each............	**tig-ápat**
five each............	**tig-limá**
ten each.............	**tig-sampû**
twenty each........	**tig-dalawampû**

*(For "**2**"&"**3**" drop the 1st letter of the number)

To add "**only**" to a number (e.g. "**only one**"),
the first syllable is reduplicated.

only one............	**íisa**
only two............	**dádalawa**
only five............	**lílima**
only ten.............	**sásampu**
only twenty.......	**dádalawampu**

For groupings (e.g. "**one by one**"), the first
two syllables are reduplicated.

one by one.......	**isa-isá**
two by two.......	**dala-dalawá**
five by five........	**lima-limá**
ten by ten.........	**sampu-sampû**

Vocabulary:

once......	**mínsan**	soon..........	**malápit na**
twice.....	**makálawa**	often..........	**madalás**
thrice.....	**maká-tatló**	seldom.......	**bihíra**

FRACTIONS & PERCENTS

Fractions are created (except 1/2) by replacing
"**IKA**"in the ika-ordinal number set with **"KA"**
Note: If the number begins with "a" - only add "k"

	Fraction Set	
a half	(1/2)	**kalahatí**
a third	(1/3)	**katló**
a fourth	(1/4)	**kápat**
a fifth	(1/5)	**kalimá**
a sixth	(1/6)	**kánim**
a seventh	(1/7)	**kapitó**
an eighth	(1/8)	**kawaló**
a ninth	(1/9)	**kasiyá**
a tenth	(1/10)	**kasampû**
		(**kapulô**)

Add cardinal numbers (followed by "**ng**") before
the fraction to create larger fractions.

two-thirds	(2/3)	**dalawáng-katló**
three-fourths	(3/4)	**tatlóng-kápat**
seven-eighths	(7/8)	**pitóng-kawaló**

For **percent** add -"**ng**" to the cardinal number
and follow it with the word "**bahagdán**".

10%	**sampúng bahagdán**
20%	**dalawampúng bahagdán**
30%	**tatlumpúng bahagdán**
40%	**apatnapúng bahagdán**
50%	**limampúng bahagdán**
60%	**animanapúng bahagdán**
70%	**pitumpúng bahagdán**
80%	**walumpúng bahagdán**
90%	**siyamnapúng bahagdán**

MONEY

The medium of exchange is the "Philippine Piso." Written "piso," pronounced "Peso," it is divided into 100 parts called centavos which are referred to as *"sentimo"* or *"sempera"* or just *"pera."*

Cultural Notes: In buying and selling, Spanish and Pilipino numbers are used indiscriminately. In rural areas both systems are used. The English system is commonly used in the Metro-Manila region.

	Pilipino	Spanish
.01	isáng sentimo	unó sempera
.02	dalawáng pera	dós sentimos
.03	tatlóng sempera	trés sentimos
.04	ápat na sentimos	kuwátro pera
.05	limáng sempera	síngko sempera
.06	ánim na pera	séis sentimos
.07	pitóng sentimos	siyéte pera
.08	walóng sempera	ótso sentimos
.09	siyám na pera	nuwébe pera
.10	sampúng sentimos	diyés sentimos
.20	dalawampúng pera	béyente sentimos
.50	sansalapi sentimos	sinkuwénta pera
1	isáng piso -or- píso	unó -or- unó píso
1.50	tatlóng salapî	unó sinkuwénta
5	limáng píso	síngko píso
10	sampúng píso	diyés píso
20	dalawampúng píso	béyente píso
50	limampúng píso	sinkuwénta píso
75	pitumpú't lima píso	seténta'y síngko
100	sandaán píso	siyénto píso
1000	isáng líbo píso	mil píso
2000	dalawang líbo píso	dós mil píso
5000	limáng líbo píso	sínko mil píso
10000	isáng yúta píso	diyés mil píso

TELLING TIME

Cultural Notes: The Spanish system dominates the Pilipino as the standard for telling time. Filipinos take a more *"relaxed"* view of punctuality than do westerners.

Vocabulary:

alá; alás	"time marker"
tangháli	noon
hátinggabí	midnight
kuwárto	quarter; 15 minutes
médya	half; 30 minutes
pára	for
y	and
óras	hour
sandalí	minute
saglít	second
Anóng óras ang ---?	What time is ---?
Anóng óras na?	What time is it?

The time marker *"alas"* is used before the hour being referred to except for one o'clock, when the time marker *"ala"* is used. Think of *"alas"* or *"ala"* as meaning *"it is"* or *"at,"* followed by the corresponding Spanish cardinal number.

Alá úna	It is one
Alás diyés	At ten
Alás dós	At two
Alás ónse	It is eleven
Alás trés	It is three
Alás dóse	At twelve
Alás dóse y média	At twelve thirty
Alá úna y kuwárto	It is one fifteen

*While conversing, should you need to indicate AM or PM, add "**ng umaga**" (morning), "**ng hapon**" (afternoon), or "**ng gabi**" (evening/night). Noon is indicated by adding "**ng tanghali**" and midnight by adding "**ng hatinggabi**" (midnight).*

Alás ótso ng umága....................	8:00 AM
Alá dose ng tanghálì..................	12:00 AM
Alá una ng hápon.......................	1:00 PM
Alás otso ng gabí.......................	8:00 PM
Alás dose ng hátinggabi.............	12:00 PM

To add minutes do as you do in English but add **"y"** *(and) between the hours and the minutes. For* "Five fifteen" *it is* ***"Sinko y kinse."*** "Six twenty" *is* ***"Seis y beynte."***

dós y diyés.................................	2:10
síngko y kawarénta y síngko.....	5:45
trés y kínse................................	3:15
séis y tréynta.............................	6:30

In English we often say **"a quarter past five"** *for* **5:15** *or* **"half past six"** *for* **6:30**. *Spanish and Pilipino have their equivalent. Instead of* **"past,"** **"y"** *(and) is used. To give a specific time use* *"impunto"* *(exactly).*

Síngko y médya..........................	5:30
Séis y kuwárto...........................	6:15

In English we use **"a quarter to six"** *for* **"five forty-five."** *Spanish and Pilipino have their equivalent but this seems to initially confuse native English speakers. In Pilipino* **"a quarter to six"** *is stated as* **"minus a quarter for six"** *(menos kuwarto para alas Seis) or* **"minus fifteen for six"** *(menos kinse para alas Seis).*

Abbreviations:

n.u. = a.m.   **n.h.** = p.m.
n.t. = noon   **n.g.** = evening

Seasons of the Philippines:

Dry...................	Nov-May..........	**"tag-inít"**
Rainy................	Jun-Oct	**"tag-ulán"**

SIGNS & GESTURES

Beckoning a person to "Come" is accomplished with a downward movement of the hand (the way westerners signifiy "go away"). Using the index finger is extremely rude.

The thumb is not used to indicate numbers. The ring and little fingers are used to indicate "two."

Pursed lips, not fingers, are used to point.

The brief raising of the eyebrows indicates "yes."

Direct & prolonged eye contact is considered rude.

Hissing -"Ssst Ssst"- is used to gain attention
              (except at social functions).

Clucking indicates annoyance, frustration, & anger.

If Filipinos don't understand a question, they will open their mouths.

A limp handshake is socially acceptable.

Members of the same sex will hold hands.

Filipinos often express their curiosity by staring and unrestrained questioning. Neither are hostile nor flattering nor offensive.

DATES

To ask about **dates** use "**petsa**" (*date*).

Q: Anóng <u>pétsa</u> ngayón?
What <u>date</u> is today?

R: <u>A-dós</u> ng Nobyémbre (ngayón).
(Today is) the <u>2</u> of November.

Q: Anóng <u>pétsa</u> ang Paskó?
What <u>date</u> is Christmas?

**R: <u>A-béynte-sínko</u> ng Disyémbre (ang
Paskó).**
(Christmas is on) December <u>25th</u>.

To ask when **events** will occur use "**kailan**"
(*when*). "<u>Kailán</u>" (*when*) questions are
answered by dates preceded by "**sa**."

Q: <u>Kailán</u> ang káarawan mó?
<u>When</u> is your birthday?

R: <u>Sa</u> a-dóse (ng Disyémbre).
<u>On</u> the 12 (of December).

Q: <u>Kailán</u> ang okasyón.?
<u>When</u> is the celebration (special event)?

R: <u>Sa</u> a-priméro.
<u>On</u> the 1.

To ask about **days** of the week use "**áraw**" (day).

Q: Anóng <u>áraw</u> ngayón?
What <u>day</u> is it today?

R; Miyérkoles (ngayón).
(Today is) Wednesday.

Q: Anóng <u>áraw</u> ba iyón?
What <u>day</u> is that?

R: Linggó
Sunday

HOLIDAYS AND EVENTS

Bataan Day	**Áraw ng Bataan**
Birthday	**Kaárawan**
Election	**Eleksiyón**
Christmas	**Paskó**
Easter	**Paskó ng Pagkabuhay**
Good Friday	**Biyérnes Santo**
Holy Week	**Mahál na Áraw**
Independence Day	**Áraw ng Kalayáan**
Lent	**Kuwarésma**
New Year	**Bágong Taón**
People Power Day	**Áraw ng Pagkakaisa ng Puwersang Pilipino**
Jose Rizal Day	**Áraw ni Jose Rizal**
Thanksgiving Day	**Áraw ng Pasasalámat**
All Saint's Day	**Áraw ng mgá Patáy**
All Soul's Day	**Áraw ng mgá Kaluluwa**
Valentine's Day	**Áraw ng mgá Púso**

DAYS OF THE WEEK
(If you know Spanish you are in luck.)

Monday.............	**Lúnes**
Tuesday............	**Martés**
Wednesday........	**Miyérkoles**
Thursday............	**Huwébes**
Friday................	**Biyérnes**
Saturday............	**Sábado**
Sunday..............	**Linggó**

MONTHS OF THE YEAR
(Same as Spanish)

January.............	**Enéro**
February............	**Pebréro**
March................	**Márso**
April..................	**Abríl**
May..................	**Máyo**
June.................	**Húnyo**
July..................	**Húlyo**
August..............	**Agósto**
September.........	**Setyémbre**
October.............	**Oktúbre**
November..........	**Nobyémbre**
December..........	**Disyémbre**

Cultural Notes: With more than 50 million people, the Philippines is home to the fifteenth largest population in the world.

Vocabulary:

date	**pétsa**
day	**áraw**
today; now	**ngayón**
right now	**ngayón din**
tomorrow	**búkas**
tomorrow morning	**búkas ng umága**
day after tomorrow	**samakalawá**
yesterday	**kahápon**
day before yesterday	**kamakalawá**
every day	**áraw-áraw**
some day	**balang áraw**
some other day	**sa ibang áraw na**
morning	**umága**
noon	**tanghalíng tapát**
afternoon	**hápon**
evening/night	**gabí**
midnight	**hatinggabí**
last night	**kagabí**
week	**linggó**
next week	**sa linggóng dárating**
last week	**ng linggóng nagdaán**
month	**buwán**
next month	**sa buwáng dárating**
last month	**ng buwáng nagdaáan**
year	**taón**
every afternoon	**tuwíng hápon**
every night	**gabí-gabí**
every Sunday	**tuwíng Linggó**
every year	**taun-taón**

BASIC VOCABULARY

Many of the Pilipino personal pronouns have two forms depending on whether they appear before the noun **(pre-)** *[regular sentence form] or after the noun* **(post-)** *[transposed sentence form].*

First person plural personal pronouns have two forms depending on whether they include the person spoken to **(inclusive - *inc*)** *or not* **(exclusive - *exc*).*

I (me)..............................	**akó**	
you *(singular)*...................	**ikáw**	*(pre-)*
....	**ká**	*(post-)*
you *(plural)*.....................	**kayó**	
he/she............................	**siyá**	
we (us)...........................	**kamí**	*(exc)*
....	**táyo**	*(inc)*
they...............................	**silá**	
my (mine)......................	**ákin**	*(pre-)*
....	**kó**	*(post-)*
your(s) *(singular)*..............	**iyó**	*(pre-)*
....	**mo**	*(post-)*
his/her(s).......................	**kaniyâ**	*(pre-)*
....	**niyá**	*(post-)*
our(s)............................	**ámin**	*(exc)(pre-)*
....	**átin**	*(inc)(pre-)*
our(s)............................	**námin**	*(exc)(post-)*
....	**nátin**	*(inc)(post-)*
your(s)...........................	**inyó**	*(pre-)*
....	**ninyó**	*(post-)*
their(s)..........................	**kanilá**	*(pre-)*
....	**nilá**	*(post-)*

by me	**ákin**	*(pre-)*
	kó	*(post-)*
by you *(singular)*	**iyó**	*(pre-)*
	mo	*(post-)*
by him/her	**kanyá**	*(pre-)*
	niyá	*(post-)*
by us	**átin**	*(inc)(pre-)*
	nátin	*(inc)(post-)*
by us	**ámin**	*(exc)(post-)*
	námin	*(exc)(post-)*
by you *(plural)*	**inyó**	*(pre-)*
by you *(plural)*	**ninyó**	*(post-)*
by them	**kanilá**	*(pre-)*
by them	**nilá**	*(post-)*
to me	**sa ákin**	
to you *(singular)*	**sa iyó**	
to him/her	**sa kanyá**	
to us	**sa átin** *(inc)*	
to us	**sa ámin** *(exc)*	
to you *(plural)*	**sa inyó**	
to them	**sa kanilá**	
for me	**pára sa ákin**	
for you *(singular)*	**pára sa íyo**	
for him/her	**pára sa kanyá**	
for us	**pára sa átin** *(inc)*	
for us	**pára sa ámin** *(exc)*	
for you *(plural)*	**pára sa inyó**	
for them	**pára sa kanilá**	
who *(singular)*	**síno**	
who *(plural)*	**sínu-síno**	
whose	**ninó**	
what	**anó**	

("**Ano**" - sometimes used as a greeting as "Hello")

when..............................	**kailán**
where (person/thing).........	**nasaán**
(act)....................	**saán**
why..............................	**bákit**
which..........................	**alín**
how..............................	**paáno**
how much......................	**magkáno**
how many......................	**Ilán**

this..............................	**itó**

(item near the person speaking)

that (there).....................	**iyán**

(item near the person spoken to)

that (over there)..............	**iyón**

(item far from person speaking and spoken to)

these.............................	**ang mgá itó**

(items near person speaking)

those.............................	**ang mgá iyán**

(items near person spoken to)

those.............................	**ang mgá iyón**

(items far from person speaking and spoken to)

Note: *In singular form* **ito**, **iyan**, & **iyon** *are not preceeded by the marker* **"ang."** *In plural form they are preceeded by* **"ang mga."**

here..............................	**díto**
there.............................	**diyán**
over there......................	**doón**
it is here.......................	**héto**
it is there......................	**hayún**

GREETINGS & INTRODUCTIONS

Grammar Notes: The respectful particle **"PO."**
In Pilipino the particle **"po"**is used as an
indication of respect (for one's elders,
superiors, and for strangers) and is roughly
equivalent to **"sir"** or **"ma'am."** This will be
referred to as **"formal"** speech. To younger
persons and to friends **"po"** is not used. This
will be referred to as the **"informal"** speech. If
you feel comfortable calling a person by his/her
first name <u>do not</u> use formal speech.
"Ho" is a less formal variation of **"po."**

"Naman" is another particle which does not
occur in colloquial English. In an expression
like **"Magandang gabi po naman"** it roughly
means "too," "also," or "to you too." In an
expression such as **"Mabuti po naman"** it is
used like "quite/pretty" as in "quite well" or
"pretty well."

Vocabulary:

Mr. is abbreviated **G.**; **Mrs.** is **Gng.**; **Miss** is **Bb.**

Mister, Mr.	**Ginóo**
Mr. Smith......................	**Ginóong** Smith
Madam, Mrs.	**Ginang**
Mrs. Smith....................	**Ginang** Smith
Miss.............................	**Binibíni**
Miss Smith....................	**Binibíning** Smith

Grammar Notes: A linker **-ng** is added to
Ginoo (Mr) and **Binibini** (Miss) when used with
names. **Ginang** (Mrs) remains the same with
or without names.

Cultural Notes*: There is no Pilipino equivalent of "**Ms.**" When addressing a woman, take your best guess. If you are wrong you will be politely corrected. To informally address a woman one does not know use "**Ale**" or "**Ali**." To informally address a man one does not know use "**Mamà**."*

Greetings

Formal:

Good morning (sir/ma'am)
Magandáng umága pô.

Good noon (sir/ma'am)
Magandáng tanghálì pô. *(1)*

Good afternoon (sir/ma'am)
Magandáng hápon pó. *(2)*

Good evening (sir/ma'am)
Magandáng gabí pô.

Good night (sir/ma'am)
Magandáng gabí pô.

Good day (sir/ma'am)
Magandáng áraw pô. *(3)*

Good morning, Mr Smith.
Magandáng umága pô G Smith.

Good afternoon, Miss Smith.
Magandáng hápon pô Bb Smith.

Good night, Mrs Smith.
Magandáng gabí pô Gng Smith.

(1) Used from 12:00 AM - 1:00 PM
(2) Used from   2:00 PM - 5:00 PM
(3) Used from sunup to sunset.

Informal:

Good morning to you.
Magandáng umága sa iyó.

Good noon to you, Carlos.
Magandáng tangháli sa iyó, Carlos.

Good afternoon to you, Linda.
Magandáng hápon sa iyó, Linda.

Good evening to you. (plural-2 or more persons)
Magandáng gabí sa inyó.

Good day to you. (plural-3 or more persons)
Magandáng áraw sa inyóng lahát.

Neutral:

Good morning
Magandáng umága.

Good noon
Magandáng tangháli.

Good afternoon
Magandáng hápon.

Good evening
Magandáng gabí.

Responses

Formal:

Good morning, also (sir/ma'am).
Magandáng umága pô namán.

Good noon to you, too (sir/ma'am).
Magandáng tanghálì pô namán.

Good day to you (sir/ma'am).
Magandáng áraw pô namán.

Good evening, too, Miss Smith.
Magandáng gabí pô namán, Bb Smith.

Good day to you, too, Mr. & Mrs. Smith.
Magandáng áraw pô namán, G at Gng Smith

Informal:

Good morning (to you).
Magandáng umága sa iyó.

Good noon (to you), Maria.
Magandáng tanghálì sa iyó, Maria.

Good evening (to you), Susy. How are you?
Magandáng gabí sa iyó, Susy. Kumustá ka?

(Magandang is from maganda (meaning nice, pretty, beautiful) plus the linker -ng.)

(Kumusta, from the Spanish "como está", means "How are you?")

Neutral:

> Good morning, too.
> **Magandáng umága namán.**

> Good afternoon to you, too.
> **Magandáng hápon namán.**

> Good evening, also.
> **Magandáng gabí namán.**

Civilities

Questions:

How are you? **Kumustá pô kayó?**
(Formal; singular & plural)

How are you? **Kumustá ka?**
(Informal; singular)

How are you (all)? **Kumustá kayó?**
(Informal; plural)

Responses:

Very well, thanks. (Formal)	**Mabúti pô namán, salámat.**
Well, thanks. And you? (Informal)	**Mabúti, salámat. At Ikáw?**
Quite well. (Informal)	**Mabúti namán.**
I'm fine. (Informal)	**Mabúti akó.**

Note: "**Kayo**", the plural of "**Ka**" (you) is used in formal speech even when addressing one person.

Questions:

> How is your husband/wife?
> **Kumustá ang iyóng asáwa?***

> How are your children?
> **Kumustá ang iyóng mgá anák?**

> How are your mother and father?
> **Kumustá ang iyóng iná at amá?**

Responses:

> Fine too, thank you.
> **Mabúti rin, salámat.**

> Fine too, by the grace of God.
> **Mabúti namán, sa awa ng Diyós.**
> *(a common response when the inquiries are made
> about family members)*

Vocabulary Note: *"**Asawa**" = husband or wife
(e.g. spouse) in this context. "Asawa" is used
colloquially for "wife" and is much more common
than the more formal "**maybahay**" (wife).

Introductions

Formal:

> Mr. and Mrs. Smith, I would like to introduce
> you to Linda, my wife.
> **G at Gng Smith, gustó kong ipakilala sa
> inyó si Linda, maybáhay ko.**

Mrs Smith, I would like to introduce you to my
wife, Susan.
Gng Smith, gustó kong ipakilala sa inyó*
ang áking** asáwa, si Susan.

Grammar Notes:
*Notice that "**inyo**" (the plural of "to you") is used for
respect (formal) even though only one person is
being addressed.

** "My" is "**aking**" when it precedes the noun and "**ko**"
when it follows.

Mr. and Mrs. Smith, I would like to introduce
you to my friends, John and Mary Doe.
G. at Gng Smith, gustó kong ipakilala sa
inyó ang mga kaibígan ko, siná John at
Mary Doe.

Informal:

Maria, I'd like to introduce you to my wife,
Suzanne.
Maria, gustó kong ipakilala sa iyó ang áking
asáwa, Suzanne.

Mary and Sam, I'd like to introduce to you
Sally, my wife.
Mary at Sam, gustó kong ipakilala sa inyó si
Sally, maybáhay ko.

Peter, I'd like to introduce you to Bob, my
husband.
Peter, gustó kong ipakilala sa iyó si Bob,
asáwa ko.

John, I'd like to introduce you to my friend,
Harry.
**John, gustó kong ipakilala sa iyó ang aking
kaibígan, si Harry.**

Neutral:

This is Carla, my wife.
Itó pô si Carla, maybáhay ko.

This is Arlene, my wife.
Itó pô si Arlene, asáwa ko.

This is Bob, my husband.
Itó pô si Bob, asáwa ko.

This is John Doe, my friend
Itó pô si John Doe, kaibígan ko.

This is Mr. Smith.
Itó pó si Ginoóng Smith.

This is Mrs. Smith.
Itó pó si Gínang Smith.

This is Miss Smith.
Itó pó si Binibíning Smith.

I am John Smith.
Akó ay si John Smith.
(Ako'y si John Smith.)

Responses

I'm pleased to meet you, Mrs. Smith.
Ikinagagalak kong mákilala kayó, Gng Smith.

I'm pleased to meet you, Mr. and Mrs. Smith.
Ikinagagalak kong mákilala kayó, G at Gng Smith.

We are pleased to meet you, Mrs. Smith.
Nagagalak kamíng mákilala kayó, Gng Smith.

We are pleased to meet you, Mr. and Mrs. Smith.
Nagagalak kamíng mákilala kayó, G at Gng Smith.

I'm (also) pleased to meet you, Susan.
Nagagalak (din) pô akóng mákilala kayó, Susan.

Likewise
Gayón din pô kamí

Grammar Notes: *"Ikinagagalak"* & *"Nagagalak"* *are two different verbs formed from the root* ***"galak"*** *meaning "happiness."* ***"Ikinagagalak kong makilala kayo"*** *translates as "That you are introduced pleases me."* ***"Nagagalak akong makilala kayo"*** *translates as "I am pleased that you are introduced." Though both say the same thing the first focuses on the cause for the feeling, the latter focuses on the feeling of the speaker.*

COMMON PHRASES

More Greetings:

Hoy
Heh; Hi

*Saán ka papuntá.
Where are you going?

*Saán ka gáling?
Where have you been?

neither actually mean what they ask - equivalent to "Hello" or "How are you." Respond with the vague "diyan lang" response meaning "over there" "just there."

More Responses:

* Diyán lang.
Over there. - Just there.

**Mabúti sa walâ.
Better than nothing.

**Héto, buháy pa.
Still alive.

**Humihinga pa.
Still breathing.

**Nakakaraos namán.
Barely surviving.

**These responses should not be taken seriously. They mean things are OK. Saying the opposite of what is meant is a common feature of Pilipino informal conversation.

Getting Acquainted:

Who are you?
Síno ba kayó?

What is your name?
Anó ang pangálan ninyó?

What are your names?
Anú-anó ba ang mga pangálan ninyó?

I am *Roger.*
Akóy si* *Roger.*

My name is *Roger.*
Ang pangálan ko ay *Roger.*

Who is your companion?
Síno ba ang kasáma mo?

This is my friend, *Sophia.*
Itóy áking kaibígan si* *Sophia.*

We are *Roger* and *Sophia.*
Kamí ay siná* *Roger* at *Sophia.*

* *Si/sina - is used to mark the topic or subject of a
sentence when it is someone's name.*

We are friends.
Táyo'y magkaibígan.

This is *Brian.*
Itó ay si *Brian.*

That is *Glenda*.
Iyán ay si *Glenda*.

They are *Brian* and *Glenda*.
Silá ay siná *Brian* at *Glenda*.

They are friends.
Silá ay magkaibígan.

I have a friend in *Baguio*.
Akó ay may kaibígan sa *Baguio*.

I have friends in *Manila*.
Akó ay may mga kaibígan sa *Maynilá*.

Where do you come from?
Taga-saáng bayán ka?

I am an *American*.
Akó ay *Amerikano*.

I came from the *United States*.
Galíng akó sa *Estados Unidos*.

I am new in the Philippines.
Bágo akó sa Pilipinas.

When did you arrive?
Kailán ka dumatíng?

Do you know *English*?
Marúnong ba kayó ng *Ingles*?

Do you speak *Tagalog*?
Nakákapagsalitá ba kayó ng *Tagálog*?

I speak only a little *Tagalog*.
Nakákapagsalitá akó ng káunting *Tagálog*.

I am learning to speak *Tagalog*.
Nag-áaral akóng magsalitâ ng *Tagálog*.

You must correct my pronunciation.
Iwastô mo ang áking bigkás.

How do you say *"Hello"* in *Tagalog*?
**Paáno mo sasábihin sa *Tagálog* ang
"Hello"?**

What is *"Hello"* in *Tagalog*?
Anó sa *Tagálog* ang "Hello"?

Where do you live (stay)?
Saán kayó nakatirá?

At the *Plaza Hotel*
Sa Otel Plaza

I live at the *Plaza Hotel*.
Nakatirá akó sa *Otel Plaza*.

Please write your name.
Pakisúlat mo ang iyóng pangálan.

Give me your address.
Ibigáy mo sa ákin ang iyóng tíráhan.

Write to me.
Sumúlat ka sa ákin.

Where is *Susan*?
Nasaán si *Susan*.

Where did *Susan* go?
Saán pumuntá si *Susan*?

Where is she (he)?
Násaán siyá?

She (he) left already.
Siyá ay umalís na.

When are you leaving?
Kailán ang alís mo?

When will you leave?
Kailán ka aalís?

Don't leave!
Huwág kang umalís!

Where shall we eat?
Saán táyo kákain?

We shall eat here.
Díto táyo kákain.

Where are you going?
Saán ka ba pupuntá?

to the *movies*.
Diyán lang sa *síne*.

Where have you been?
Saán ka ba galing?

Are you going home now?
Uuwî ka na ba ngayón?

Can you return tomorrow?
Makabábalík ba kayó búkas?

I shall return tomorrow.
Magbábalík akó búkas.

(You) Wait for me!
Maghintáy ka sa ákin!

I will wait for you.
Híhintayín kita.

I'll be back at *two* o'clock.
Bábalík akó ng alas *dos*.

so long
O, sige na.

goodbye
"Paalam" - "Adyios"

"Paalam" is the formal "goodbye." It is used by the
person leaving first. "**Adiyos**" is used as a response
to"**Paalam**."

SMALL TALK

Come here!
Halíka díto!

How old are you?
Iláng taón ka na?

Where do you come from?
Tagásaang bayán ka?

I like you.
Gustó kitá.

You are very kind.
Nápakabuti mo.

You are beautiful.
Magandá ka.

I like this.
Gustó ko itó.

I don't like *(this)*.
Ayaw ko *itó*. (Ayóko itó.)

Do you like this?
Gustó mo ba íto?

What do you like?
Ano ba ang gustó mo? (Anóng gusto mo?)

I don't know.
Áywan ko. (Hindî ko alam.)

Do you know him/her?
Kilála mo ba siyá?

Who is he/she?
Síno ba siyá?

What did you say?
Anóng sinábi mo?

It is up to you.
Bahála ka.

happen what may
Bahála na

may it be so
Káhimanawarí

once in a while
Kung mínsan

later on
Saká na

later on (today)
Mamayá na

Is it true?
Totoô ba?

Are you sure?
Siguradó ka ba?

not so
Hindî namán

So what!
Mano!

Never mind!
Hindî bále!

I do not have time.
Walâ akóng panahón.

It's too late.
Hulí na.

It's none of your business.
Walâ kang pakíalam.

What a pity.
Sáyang.

It's all right. (It's enough)
Táma na.

I understand.
Naintindihán ko.

I do not understand.
Hindî ko naintindihán.

Come with me!
Sumáma ka sa ákin!

I'll be going now.
Aalís na akó.

Get lost.
Alís diyán.

Let's go.
Tena.

not yet.
Walâ pa

Wait a moment.
Hintáy ka. (Teka! *or* **Sandali!)**

(You) be quick.
Madali ka. (Dalíka!)

just a moment
Sandalí lámang

Be quick, we will be late.
Dalíka, mahuhulî táyo.

Go on!
Síge na.

Are you coming (along)?
Sásama ka ba?

perhaps
Maráhil

maybe
Sigúro

Why are you sad?
Bákit ka ba malungkot?

What are you worring about?
Ano ang ináalaala mo?

Please sit down.
Maupo ka.

Stop it! -or- Shut up!
Tama ka na! *(Mild & Polite)*

Go to sleep.
Túlog na.

Wake up.
Gísing na.

B.S.
Bolabola

O.K.
Síge

It's late. Let's go home.
Gabí na. Táyo ng umuwí.

HELP ME *(Tulungán mo akó)*

What is this?
Anó ba itó?

What is that?
Anó ba iyán?

Do you have *(cigarettes; matches)*?
Mayroón bang *(sigarilyo; posporo)*?

Where can I find a *telephone*?
.......*mechanic?*
......*policeman?*

Saán may *telepono*?
......*mechaniko*?
......*pulis*?

Where is the *mailbox*?
......*market?*
........*toilet?*

Nasaán ang *buson*?
......*palenke*?
.......*kasilyas*?

I cannot speak Tagalog.
Hindî akó marunong ng Tagalog.

Can anyone here speak *English*?
Mayroón ba ritong marunong ng *Ingles*?

Call someone who can speak *English*.
Tumáwag ka ng isáng marunong ng *Ingles*.

I want to speak to the *manager*.
Gustó kong mákausap ang *mánedyer*.

Are you the *manager*?
Ikáw (Kayó) ba ang *mánedyer*?

Can the *driver* speak *English*?
Marunong ba ng *Ingles* ang *tsupér*?

When can I speak to the *owner*?
Kailán ko puwedeng makáusap ang *may-ári*?

When will he return?
Anóng oras ang balík niyá

I'll wait!
Maghíhintáy akó!

I'll return later.
Bábalík akó mámayâ.

May I use your *telephone*?
**Puwéde bang makigamit ng inyóng
telépono?**

Hello, is this number *123-4567*?
Haló! Itó ba ang número *123-4567*?

Will you please call this number?
**Pakítawagon mo ngá ang númerong
ito para sa ákin?**

May I speak with *Mr. Smith*?
Puwéde bang makausap si *Ginóo Smith*?

Please tell him that I called.
Pakísabi mo lamang na akó'y tumáwag.

Please tell him to call me when he returns.
**Pakísabi mo lamang na tawagan
akó pagbalík niyá.**

Hold the line.
Huwág mo munang ibábabá ang telépono.

speak louder
Pakilaksán lang ng kauntí ang boses mo

Cultural Notes:

"Pakikisama" - *art of smooth social transactions.
Filipinos believe that relationships should not have
open conflict. Lack of courtesy or consideration is
perceived as a challenge to personal honor. Take
care not to be critical or sarcastic or play practical
jokes that embarrass individuals in front of others.*

"Hiya" - *sensitivity to social propriety. Filipinos will
go to great lengths to avoid causing others* **hiya**
(shame or embarassment).

Amor Propio - *self esteem. Filipinos are expected
to be sensitive to the feelings of others so that the
self esteem of others is not hurt. Filipinos are more
easily offended than westerners. Apologies do not
always repair the damage.*

OUT AND ABOUT

How do I get to *Makati* from here?
Paáno ang papuntá sa *Makati*?

Is this the way to *Roxas Avenue*?
Itó ba ang daang patungo sa *Avenida Roxas*?

Show me the way.
Iturò mo sa ákin ang daán.

Come with me!
Sumama ka sa ákin!

Will you come with me?
Sásáma ka ba sa ákin?

Call a taxi.
Tumawag ka ng taksi.

Call a taxi for me.
Itawag mo akó ng isáng taksi.

How much to the *Peninsula Hotel*?
Magkáno sa *Otél Peninsula*?

How much is the fare to the *hotel*?
Magkáno ang pamásahe sa *otel*?

Take me to the *Mandarin Hotel*.
Dalhín mo akó sa *Otél Mandarin*.

Take us to the *bank*.
Dalhín mo kamí sa *bangko*.

How far is it?
Gaanó kalayò itó?

How far is it from here?
Gaanó kalayò iyón búhat díto?

How many kilometers to *Cavite*?
Iláng kilómetró hanggáng *Cavite*?

How long will it take to get there ?
Iláng oras ang papuntá doón ?

Does a *bus* stop here?
Tumítigil ba rito ang *bús*?

Where is the *bus station*?
Nasáan ang *estasyón ng bús*?

Where is the *bus stop*?
Nasaán ang *hintayan ng bús*?

How long before a *bus* comes?
Gaanóng katagál ang datíng ng *bús*?

Where do I catch the *bus* to *Manila*?
Nasaán ang sákáyan ng *bús* sa *Maynilà*?

Which is the *bus* for *Cavite*?
Alíng *bús* ang papuntáng *Cavite*?

Where does this *bus* go?
Saán papuntá ang *bús* na itó?

Where do I get off?
Saán akó dápat bumabâ?

What time will we arrive in *Manila*?
Anóng oras ang datíng sa *Maynilà*?

Where is the *ticket office*?
Nasaán ang *kuhanán ng tiket*?

Is this the *train* to *Manila*?
Itó ba ang ng *trén* sa *Maynilà*?

When is the next *train* to *Manila*?
**Anóng oras ang datíng ng súsunód
na *trén* para sa *Maynilà*?**

Is this a through *train* to *Manila*?
**Ang *trén* bang itó'y tuluy-tulóy hanggáng
Maynilà?**

I want to reserve a seat.
Íbig kong magparesérba ng isáng úpúan.

What is the fare?
Magkáno ang báyad?

Give me a *1st / 2d / 3d* class ticket.
**Bigyán mo akó ng tiket na de
primera/segunda/tersera clase.**

Here is my baggage.
Héto ang kargáda ko.

There are *three* pieces.
May *tatlóng* piráso.

This is mine.
Ákin itó.

What town is this?
Anóng báyan itó?

Where do I catch the *jeepney*?
Nasaán ang sásakáy ng *dyípni*?

Meet me at the station at *two* o'clock.
Magkíta táyo sa estasyón ng alas-*dos*.

We will go back now.
Bábalík na kamí.*

We must get back by *two* o'clock.
Kailángang bumalík táyo* ng alas-*dos*.

* *Kami* if person spoken to is excluded, *Tayo* if included.

Conveyances:

airplane	**eropláno**
automobile; car	**awtò; kótse**
boat; canoe	**bangkâ**
bicycle	**bisikléta**
bus	**bús**
cart	**karitón**
horse drawn rig	**karitéla; kalésa**
jeepney	**dyípni**
motorcycle	**motorsíklo**
raft	**balsá**
ship	**barkó**
taxi	**táksi**
train	**trén**
tricycle	**traysíkel**
truck	**trák**

PLACES *(Mga lugar)*

airport	airport; palipáran
auto repair	talyér ng áwto
bakery	panaderyá
bank	bángko
barber shop	barberyá
beauty parlor	pakulútan
bus station	estasyón ng bus
cafeteria; cafe	kapetiryá
carnival; fair	karnabál
carpenter shop	karpinteriá
cathedral	katedrál
casino	"casino"; sugálan
catholic church	iglesia katólika
cemetery	sementéryo
church	iglesya; simbáhan
churchyard	pátyo
clinic	klínika
cobbler	sapátero
cock (fight) pit	sabungán; galleras
consulate	konsúl
convent	kumbénto
dormitory	dormitóryo
dressmaker	modísta
drugstore	botíka
embassy	embaháda
funeral home	punerárya
garage	garáhe
gas station	gasolínahan
grocery store	groseri
hospital	ospitál
hotel	otél
night club	naitkláb
office	opisína

parking place	**paradahán**
pharmacy	**parmásya**
pier; port; warf	**piyér; daúngan**
playground	**palarúan**
post office	**koreo; pos ópis**
restaurant	**restawrán**
-Chinese	**pansiteryá**
school	**eskuela/paaralán**
-elementary	**mabábang paaralán**
-high school	**mataás na paaralán**
-college	**koléhiyo**
-university	**universidád**
store	**tindáhan**
-book	**"" ng aklát**
-clothing	**"" ng damít**
-hardware	**"" ng hardwer**
-jewelry	**"" ng aláhas**
-shoe	**"" ng sapátos**
-stationary	**"" ng papél**
street corner	**kánto**
supermarket	**supermarket**
synagogue	**sinagoga**
tailor shop	**sastré**
telephone	**telépono**
terminal	**terminal**
town/city	**bayán/lungsód**
town hall	**munisípyo**
town square	**plása**
train station	**estasyón ng tren**
variety store	**sári-sári**
village	**barangáy**
watchmaker	**relohéro**
warehouse	**bodéga**

MOTORING

Is this a good road?
Mabúti bang daán itó?

Can I park my car here?
Puwéde ko bang iparáda dito ang áking kótse?

Is this the way to *San Jóse*?
Itó ba angdaáng patungo sa *San Jóse*?

Will you show me the way on the map?
Ituró mo ngá sa ákin sa mápang itó ang daán?

How far is it from here?
Gaáno kalayó iyón búhat díto?

Is there a good hotel at *San Miguel*?
Mayroón bang mabúting ótel sa *San Miguel*?

My car is stalled!
Tumígil ang kótse ko!

Will you send for a mechanic?
Magpaparíto ka ngá ng isáng mekániko?

Is there a repair shop near here?
May talyér ba ng áwto sa malápit dito?

Can you repair my car right now?
Puwéde mo bang kumpunihín agád ang kótse ko?

What will you charge?
Magkáno ang singíl ninyó?

Will you send one of your men to get it?
**Puwéde bang ipakuha ninyó iyón sa isa
ninyóng tao?**

When can I have it?
Kailán ko mákukuha ang kótse?

Will you wash my car?
Húgasan mo nga ang áking kótse.

Give me *twenty* liters.
Bigyán mo akó ng *beinte* litro.

turn/go left	**kumaliwá**
turn/go right	**kumanán**
to/on the left	**sa kaliwá**
to/on the right	**sa kanán**
straight	**deretso**
go straight	**dumeretso**
Stop!	**Pára!**
stop at the *corner*	**pára sa *kánto***

not so fast
Huwág masyádong matúlin

Drive slower.
Bágalan mo ng kauntí ang pagpapatakbó.

AT THE HOTEL *(Otél)*

Useful Phrases:

I would like a room.
Gustó kong kumuha ng isáng kuwárto.

a room with *one* bed
Isáng kuwártong may *isáng* kama.

a room with *two* bed (*s*)
Isáng kuwártong may *dalawáng* kama.

a room with a private bath
Isáng kuwártong may saríling bányo.

I would like a smaller room.
Gustó kong isang mas maliit na kuwárto.
(Gustó kong isang maliit-liít na kuwárto.)

What is the cost per *day*? (-*week*; -*month*)
Magkáno ang bayad bawat *araw*?
(-*lingo*; -*buwan*)

I'll take the room.
Sige kukúnin ko ang kuwártong ito.

Will you get my baggage?
Pakikuha mo nga ang áking kargáda?

I want another *blanket*.
Gustó ko ng isá pang *kúmot*.

I am expecting a visitor.
May dárating akóng bisíta.

Send him (her) up.
Papanhikín mo siya.

Ask him (her) to wait.
Sábihin mong maghintáy.

I will be right down.
Bábabá akó ngayón din.

I am leaving *today* (*tomorrow*).
Áalis akó *ngayón* (*búkas*).

I want my clothes washed.
Gustó kong magpalabá ng damít.

When can I have them back?
Kailán maibábalik ang mga itó?

Be careful with this!
Pag-ingatan mo itó.

This is not mine.
Hindí ákin itó.

There are a few pieces missing.
May náwawaglít na iláng piráso.

Please sew buttons on this.
Pakilagyán mo lámang ng butónes itó.

I want this mended.
Gustó kong itoý másulsihan.

Please clean the room.
Pakilinis ang kuwárto.

Vocabulary:

bathroom	**bányo**
bed	**káma**
bed spread	**kubrekáma**
blanket	**kúmot**
child's bib	**bibero**
curtain	**kurtína**
diaper	**lampín**
key	**susí**
mosquito net	**kulambó**
pillow	**únan**
pillow case	**pundá**
restroom	**comfort room "CR"; kubeta**
room	**kuwárto**
sheet	**kúmot**
shampoo	**shampoo**
soap	**sabón**
toilet	**kasílyas; pálikurán**
toothpaste	**colgate**
towel	**tuwálya**
washcloth	**labakara bimpo**

Cultural Notes: The Philippines has one of the highest literacy rates in Asia. About 90% of the population speaks, reads, and writes at least one language. Many older Filipinos are bilingual (local language or dialect & English) and many younger Filipinos are trilingual (local language or dialect, English & Pilipino). English remains the most useful language for formal communication and is employed by professionals, government workers, academics, and businessmen. Spanish, once the language of the upper class, is spoken by less than one million people, mostly members of the social elite.

SHOPPING

Where can I buy some *gifts*?
Saán akó makákabilí ng *mgá pangregalo*?

Do you have *cigarettes*?
Mayroón ba kayóng *sigarilyo*?

Do you have any *beer*?
Mayroón ba kayong *serbésa*?

Is this made in the Philippines?
Gawá ba rito sa Pilipinas itó?

Do you like this?
Gustó mo ba itó?

What do you like?
Anóng gustó mo?

I will try that one.
Súsubukin ko ang isáng iyán.

I will try this on.
Isúsukat ko itó.

This one is rather tight.
Ang isáng íto'y párang masikíp.

The sleeves seem tight.
Parang makipot ang manggás.

This does not appear to fit well.
Párang hindî lápat itó.

It's too loose around the waist.
Nápakaluwáng sa bandáng baywanag.

Extend the sleeves a little.
Aryahán mo nang kauntí ang manggás.

Will this shrink?
Hindî ba itó úurong?

Will the color fade?
Hindî ba kúkupas ang kulay?

That one is fine.
Pino ang isáng iyán.

I want this one.
Gustó ko ang isáng itó.

I want that one.
Gustó ko ang isáng iyán?

How much?
Magkáno?

How much for everything?
Magkáno bang lahát?

How much is this?
Magkáno ba itó?

How much is that?
Magkáno ba iyán

That is too much!
Nápakamahál namán!

Do you have anything cheaper?
Mayroón bang mas múra?

I will buy this.
Bíbilhin ko itó.

Your price is fair.
Mabúti ang halagá ninyó.

When will it be ready?
Kailán matatápos?

When will you have it finished?
Kailán mo matatápos itó?

I'll come back for it tomorrow *(afternoon)*.
Babalikan ko iyán bukas *(ng hapon)*.

Please wrap the package.
Pakibálot ngá ninyó.

This is not the correct change.
Hindî táma ang suklí.

Vocabulary:

all	lahát
broken	sirá
few; several	kauntí
less	tamá na
many	marámi
more	kauntí pa
new *(things)*	bágo
old *(things)*	lumá
too expensive	masyádong mahál

Vocabulary:

Note: Adding the adverb **"mas"** (more) before the adjectives listed below changes the comparative degree of the adjective (e.g. **fine** *(pino)* - **finer** *(mas pino)*; **cheap** *(mura)* - **cheaper** *(mas mura)*.

cheap	**múra**
fine	**píno**
heavy	**mabigát**
large	**malakí**
light *(weight)*	**magaán**
long	**mahabá**
loose	**maluwág**
narrow	**makitíd**
short	**maigsí; maiklí**
small	**maliít**
strong *(durable)*	**matibáy**
thick	**makapál**
tight	**masikíp**
wide	**malapád**

Referring to color:

bright	**matingkád**
dull	**pusyàw**

COLORS *(Mga kulay)*

black	**itím**
-very black	**itím na itím**
blue	**asúl**
-navy blue	**asúl na asúl**
-light blue	**asúl na murà**
brown	**kapé; tsokólate**

gray	**grís; ábo**
green	**bérde**
-dark green	**bérdeng-bérde**
-light green	**bérdeng-murà**
-apple green	**bérdeng-mansánas**
-moss green	**bérdeng-lúmot**
orange	**órends; órens; dalandán**
purple	**púrpura; ubé; ubí**
pink	**rósas**
red	**pulá**
bright red	**puláng-pulá**
-scarlet	**iskarlata**
tan	**balat**
violet	**líla; úbe; ubí; biyoleta**
white	**putí**
-creme colored	**kúlay kréma**
yellow	**diláw**
-bright yellow	**diláw na diláw**
-pale yellow	**diláw na murà**

CLOTHING (Damít)

bathing suit	**báting sut;** **damít pampalígo**
blouse	**blúsa**
brassiere; bra	**brasiyér; bra**
dress	**barò; bestído**
(outer garment)	**bestído**
(national dress/costume)	**térno (formal);** **balintawák**
girdle; corset	**korsé**
jacket	**dyáket**
jeans; blue jeans	**dyins; maóng**

night gown	**nayt-gawn;**
	damít na pantúlog
pajamas	**padyáma**
panties; underpants	**pántis, pánty**;
	salawál
pants (trousers)	**pantalón**
pants (shorts)	**kórto**
raincoat	**kapóte**
robe	**roba**
shirt (with collar)	**kamisadéntro**
(collarless)	**kamisatsína**
(national dress shirt	**baróng tagálog;**
-long sleeved -formal)	**baróng**
(short sleeved- casual)	**pólo baróng**
shirt, polo	**pólosert; pólo**
shoes	**sapátos**
shawl, shoulder-kerchief	**panyuélo**
slacks	**islák**
skirt; long dress skirt	**pálda; sáya**
slip (half slip)	**hap-slíp; nágwas**
slip; chemise	**kamisón**
slippers (for dress wear)	**sapatílyas; stép-in**
slippers (for house wear)	**tsinélas**
socks; stockings	**médyas**
socks (men's)	**médyas ng laláki**
stockings (women's)	**médyas ng babáe**
suit (men's)/sports coat	**amerikána**
sweater	**swéter**
t-shirt	**t-sirt; iskíper**
undershirt	**kamiséta; sándo**
undershorts; drawers	**karsonsílyo;**
	kalsonsílyo

ACCESSORIES

belt	**sinturón**
brooch	**alpilér; bruts**
brush (hair)	**bras (sa buhók)**
buttons	**butónes**
cane	**bastón**
comb	**sukláy**
earrings	**híkaw**
gloves	**guántes**
hairpin	**aguhílya**
handbag; bag; purse	**kartamunéda; bag; portamonéda**
handkerchief	**panyó; panyolíto**
hat	**sumbréro, sumbléro**
lipstick	**lípistik**
perfume	**pabangó**
pipe	**pípa**
pomade	**pomáda**
powder	**pólbo; pulbós**
razor (shaver)	**pang-áhit**
razor (straight)	**labáha**
ring	**singsíng**
scarf	**bandána**
tie	**kurbáta**
toothbrush	**sipílyo**
umbrella	**páyong**
wallet	**wálet; pitáka**
wig	**pelúka**
wrap; shawl	**balábal; abrígo**
wristwatch	**reló; relós**

Terminology:

pleats	**piléges**
pocket	**bulsá**

AT THE RESTAURANT *(Restawrán)*

Useful Phrases:

I would like a table for *two...three.*
**Gustó ko'y isáng mésa para sa
daláwa..tatlo.**

I want a table by the window.
**Gustó ko'y isáng mésang malapit sa
bintaná.**

I would like a glass of *cold water.*
**Íbig ko sana'y isáng basong *túbig na
malamíg.***

A *glass of water*, please.
Isáng *básong túbig* ngá.

Do you want some more *water?*
Gustó mo pa ba ng *túbig.*

How much is one *coffee?*
Magkáno ang isáng *kapé?*

Give me a menu.
Ákina ang menú.

I am thirsty.
Nauúhaw akó.

We would like more *tea.*
Íbig pa námin ng *tsá.*

I am hungry.
Gutóm akó.

I'm not hungry.
Walâ akóng gana.

Give me some *bread*.
Bigyán mo akó nang *tinápay*.

I want *adobo and noodles*.
Gustó ko ng *adóbo at pansít*.

I want *fried fish and rice*.
Gustó ko ng *prítong isdá at kánin*.

I did not order this.
Hindí akó nag-order nitó.

Bring me another *salad*.
Bigyán mo akó nang isá pang *ensaláda*.

Please bring some more *fish*.
Kumúha pa kayó ng *isdá*.

just a little
Kauntí lámang

Please pass the *rice*.
Bigyán mo ako ng *kánin*.

Please bring the *dessert*.
Pakidalá mo ang *matamís*.

Take this away. It's enough.
Alisín mo na itó. Táma na.

No more, thank you.
Huwág na, salámat.

I am full.
Busóg na akó.

I have finished.
Tapós na akó.

That is plenty.
Marámi iyán.

We are through eating.
Tapós na táyong kumáin.

Please clear the table.
Pakiligpít mo na ang mésa.

That was a good meal.
Ang saráp ng pagkaín.

Bring me the (my) bill.
Ákina ang kuwénta (ko).

Vocabulary:

breakfast	**almusál**
lunch	**tanghalían**
dinner	**hapúnan**
snack	**merienda**
sandwich	**sánwits**
salad	**ensaláda**
soup	**sópas**
dessert; sweets	**matamís**
bread	**tinápay**
butter	**mantekíla**
cheese	**késo**
ice cream	**sorbetes**
sugar	**asúlkal**
salt	**asín**

pepper	**pamintá**
syrup	**pulót**

Utensils:

knife	**kutsílyo**
fork	**tinidór**
spoon	**kutsára**
teaspoon	**kutsaríta**
glass	**báso**
cup	**tása**
saucer	**platíto**
bowl	**mangkók**
plate	**pláto**
platter	**bandehádo**
pitcher	**pitsél**
napkin	**serbilyéta**
table cloth	**mantél; tapéte**
can opener	**abreláta**

Cooking Terms:

bake	**ihurnó**
blanch	**banlián**
boil	**pakuluín**
chop	**tadtarín**
cut *(with knife)*	**hiwáin**
cut *(with scissors)*	**gupitín**
broil; roast	**iníhaw**
fry	**ipiríto; pritúhin**
sauté	**igisá**
steam	**pasingawán**

BEVERAGES   *(Mga inúmin)*

beer	**serbésa**
chocolate	**tsokoláte**
coca-cola	**kok**
coffee	**kape**
ice, ice cubes	**yélo**
juice	**dyús**
lemonade	**limunáda**
liquor, wine	**álak**
local beer	**San Miguel**
milk	**gátas**
native liquor (coconut)	**lambanóg**
native liquor (palm -cane)	**tubâ**
tea	**tsa, tsaá**
water	**túbig**

INGREDIENTS and CONDIMENTS
(mga lahok at mga rekado)

bay leaves	**lawrél**
catsup	**kétsap**
cinnamon	**kanéla**
cornstarch	**gawgáw**
coconut milk	**gatá**
fish sauce	**patís**
flour	**arína; harína**
garlic	**báwang**
ginger	**lúya**
honey	**pulot-pukyutan**
mayonnaise	**mayonésa**
MSG	**bétsin**
mushrooms (black, dried)	**téngang-dagá**
mustard	**mustása**
mustard (dry)	**pulbós ng mustása**

nutmeg, anise	**anís**
oregano, marjoram	**orígano**
paprika	**pamintón**
pepper	**pamintá**
peppercorn	**pamintang buô**
salt; saltpeter	**asín; salítre**
sesame seed	**lingá**
shortening	**mantíka**
soy sauce	**tóyo**
sugar; unrefined sugar	**asúkal; panutsá**
sugar, (brown)	**puláng asúkal**
vanilla	**banílya**
vinegar	**súka**
worcestershire sauce	**sálsa perín**

MEAT *(Karne)*

beef steak	**bisték**
boiled beef	**inihaw na kárne**
beef	**kárne ng baka**
corned beef	**kárne nórte**
roast beef	**kárneng asado**
stewed beef	**kárneng gisado**
broiled beef	**nilagang kárne**
jerky	**tápa**

POULTRY *(Manukan)*

boiled fertilized egg	**balút**
chicken	**manók**
duck	**páto; bíbe**
duck egg, boiled	**pénoy**
egg, soft boiled	**itlógmalasádong itlóg**
egg; fried egg	**itlóg; prítong**
gizzard	**balún-balúnan**

omelet	**tórta**
quail	**púgo**
turkey	**pábo**

PORK *(Karneng-Baboy)*

bacon	**békon; tusíno**
BBQ pork (very fat)	**liyémpo**
(belly)	**(sa tiyán)**
feet; knuckles	**pata**
ham	**hamón**
pork rind	**sitsarón**
roast pig	**litsón**
salted pork	**karníng-baboy**
sausage	**soriso;**
	longganísa
skin	**balát**
spareribs	**tadyáng**
tenderloin	**lómo**
tripe	**góto**

SEAFOOD / FISH
(Pagkaing Galing sa Dagat /Isda)

adult mullet	**bának**
anchovy	**dílis**
black tailed caesio	**dalágang- búkid**
blue surgeon fish	**labahíta**
catfish (freshwater)	**hitò**
catfish (saltwater)	**kandulì**
cavalla	**talakítok**
clam	**halaán**
cod	**bakaláw**
crab (small)	**talangkâ**

crab (large, black)	**alimángo**
crab (speckled)	**alimásag**
dried-salted fish	**tuyô**
goby	**bía**
herring	**tambán**
immature mullet	**kapak**
lobster	**uláng**
milk fish	**bangús**
mud fish	**dalág; bulíg**
mullet	**talílong**
mussel	**tahóng**
oyster	**talabá**
pompano	**pompanó**
porgy	**bakóko**
prawn	**sugpô**
red snapper	**máya-máya**
salty fish or shrimp relish/paste	**bagoóng**
sardines	**sardínas**
seaweed	**damóng-dágat**
shark	**patíng**
shrimp	**hípon**
smoked fish	**tinapá**
sole	**dapâ**
Spanish mackerel	**tangginggì; tanigì**
spotted rock bass	**lápu-lápu**
striped mackerel	**alumáhan**
tilapia	**tilapyâ**
tuna	**tulíngan**
two fin sea bass	**apáhap**

VEGETABLES *(Mga gulay)*

bamboo shoots	**labóng**
banana heart	**pusò ng ságing**
bean sprouts	**tóge**

beans in soy sauce	**tawsí**
beets	**bits; remolátsa**
bittermelon (amargoso)	**ampalayá**
cabbage	**repólyo**
carrot	**kérot; sanórya**
cassava	**kasabá**
cauliflower	**kóliplór; kóliplawer**
chayote	**sayóte**
chestnuts	**kastányas**
chili pepper	**labúyo**
Chinese celery	**kintsáy**
Chinese cabbage	**pétsay**
corn	**maís**
cucumber	**pipíno**
eggplant	**talóng**
garbanzo bean	**garbánsos**
garlic	**báwang**
ginger	**lúya**
green pepper	**síli; síle**
horseradish	**malunggáy**
hyacinth bean	**bátaw**
lentils	**lentéhas**
lettuce	**litsúgas**
lima or kidney bean	**patáni**
mung bean	**munggó**
mushroom	**kabuté**
mustard	**mustása**
okra	**ókra**
onion	**sibúyas**
palm tree pith	**úbod**
peas	**gisántes**
potatoes	**patátas**
radish	**labanós**
scallions	**sibúyas na múra**

snap bean	**abitsuwéla**
snow pea	**sitsaró**
soy bean	**balátong**
spinach (native)	**kulítis**
sponge gourd	**patóla**
squash, pumpkin	**kalabása**
string bean	**sítaw**
sweet potato; yam	**kamóte**
taro (a starchy root)	**gábi; gábe**
tomato	**kamátis**
water chestnut	**apúlid**
watercress	**kangkóng**
wax gourd	**kondól**
white squash	**úpo**
winged beans	**sigadílyas**
yam (violet in color)	**úbi; úbe**
yam (native turnip)	**singkamás**

FRUITS *(Mga prutas)*

almond	**alméndras; ámon**
apples	**mansánas**
avacado	**abokádo**
banana (var.)	**latundán**
banana	**ságing**
banana (var.)	**lakatán**
banana (var.)	**bungúlan**
breadfruit	**rímas**
cantaloupe; melon	**milón**
cashew nut	**kasúy**
chestnut	**kastányas**
chicle	**chico**
chico (var.)	**mabúlo**
chico (var.)	**lansónes**
chico (var.)	**ponderosa**

chico (var.)	sinigwélas; tsíko
chico (var.)	duryán
chico (var.)	piera
coconut	niyóg
coconut (full of soft meat)	makapunó
cooking banana	sabá
custard apple	átis
durian	duriyán
grapes	úbas
green mango	manggáng-hiláw
guamachile	kamatsilé
guava	bayábas
half-ripe mango	manggáng-manibaláng
jackfruit	langká
Java apple	mokópa
Java plum; plum	dúhat
lemon	limón
lime	dáyap
lychee	letsíyas
magosteen	mangustín
mango	manggá
orange (var.)	dalanghíta
orange (var.)	dalandán
orange (native)	naranghíta; dalanghíta
papaya	papáya
peanuts	maní
pears	péras
pickled mango	burúng- manggá
pineapple	pinyá
pomelo	suhâ
rambutan	rambután
ripe mango	manggáng-hinog
santol	santól

small lime	**kalamansí**
soursop	**guayabáno**
star apple	**kaymíto; kaimíto**
starfruit	**balimbíng**
tamarind	**sampálok**
tangerine	**sintúnis**
velvet apple	**mabólo**
watermelon	**pakwán**
young coconut	**búko**

LOCAL FARE

Cultural Notes: Pilipino meals are not served in courses. The whole meal, served at room temperature, is laid out at once.

Adobo	*A favorite Pilipino meat dish cooked in vinegar, salt, garlic, pepper, and soy sauce.*
Am	*Rice broth*
Ampan	*Sugared popcorn*
Ampaw	*Puffed rice or corn*
Apa	*Thin rolled wafer of rice, starch, & red pepper; an ice cream cone*
Bagoong	*Salted small fish or shrimp; anchovies; shrimp relish*
Balut	*Local delicacy - boiled duck egg with partially developed embryo*
Basi	*Rice wine*
Batog	*Shelled & boiled salted corn with grated coconut*
Batsoy	*Chopped & sauteed pig entrails with soup*
Bibingka	*Baked rice cake with coconut milk and sugar*
Bihon	*Rice noodles*

Binatog	*Steamed or boiled salted corn mixed with grated coconut*
Bistik	*Thin sliced beef with soy sauce, lemon, & sliced onion*
Bukayo	*Grated coconut cooked with sugar*
Dinuguan	*Sauteéd meat and pork blood stew with spices*
Empanada	*Meat pie*
Halo-halo	*A dessert of sweetened fruits & crushed ice*
Kanin	*Boiled or steamed rice*
Kutsinta	*Steamed brown cake served with fresh coconut*
Leche Flan	*A sweet custard dish*
Liyempo	*BBQ pork; lots of fat*
Longganisa	*Pork sausage*
Lumpiya	*Meat, shrimp, and/or vegetables packed in rice starch paper*
Lugaw	*Rice porridge; watery rice*
Mamon	*A type of sponge cake*
Morkon	*Meat roll stuffed with olives, pickles, sausage, & hard boiled eggs*
Palitaw	*Rice cake made with glutinous rice, sugar, & grated coconut*
Pandisal	*A kind of "French" bread*
Pansit Molo	*A chow mein type dish*
Penoy	*Hard-boiled duck egg*
Putsero	*Boiled meat & vegetables*
Puto	*Native rice cake*
Rellenong Manok	*Chicken stuffed with hard boiled eggs, pork, sausages, and spices*
Relyeno	*Stuffed chicken, fish, or crab*
Sinangag	*Fried rice*

Siyopaw	*Steamed rice cake with meat or condiments inside*
Suman	*Native rice cake wrapped in banana or palm leaves*
Tsampurado	*Chocolate flavored porridge*

FAMILY & FRIENDS
(Pamílya at mgá kaibígan)

mother	iná
father	amá
mommy	nanáy; ináy
daddy	tátay; itáy
husband	asáwa
wife	maybáhay
spouse	asáwa
my husband	ang áking táo
my wife	ang áking maybáhay
child (in general)	batá
child (own)	anák
son	anák na laláki
daughter	anák na babáe
brother	kapatíd (na laláki)
sister	kapatíd (na babáe)
elder brother	kúya
elder sister	áte
youngest child	bunsô
eldest child	pangánay
grandfather	lólo
grandmother	lóla
grandchild	apó
grandson	apó na laláki
granddaughter	apó na babáe
father-in-law	biyanáng laláki
mother-in-law	biyanáng babáe

brother-in-law	**bayáw**
sister-in-law	**hípag**
aunt / uncle	**tiyá / tiyó**
cousin	**pínsan**
nephew	**pamangkínglaláki**
niece	**pamangkíng babáe**
man (person)	**táo**
man/male	**laláki**
woman/female	**babáe**
parents	**magúlang**
widow(er)	**bálo; báo**
mistress	**kerída; babái**
single man / woman	**bináta / dalága**
fiancé/fiancée	**nóbyo(a)**
sweetheart	**kasintáhan**
boy	**bátang laláki**
girl	**bátang babáe**
twins	**kambal**
small boy	**tótoy**
small girl	**néne**
godfather (of one's child)	**kompádre**
godmother (of one's child)	**komádre**
godfather	**nínong**
godmother	**nínang**
godchild	**inaanák**
godson	**inaanák na laláki**
goddaughter	**inaanák na babáe**
godbrother	**kinakapatíd ng-**
godsister	**- lakáki / babáe**
relative	**kamag-ának**
friend	**kaibígan**
neighbor	**kápit-báhay**
invited guest	**kumbidádo**
visitor; guest	**panaúhin**

classmate	**kaeskuwél**
partner	**kaánib**
namesake	**tokáyo**
(having same first name)	

THE HOME *(Ang Tahanan)*

apartment	**apartment**
awning	**medyá-ágwa**
backyard	**likód-báhay**
balcony	**balcón**
bathroom	**bányo**
ceiling	**kísame**
corner	**súlok**
dining room	**kumedór**
door	**pintô**
doorway	**pintúan**
downstairs	**ibabá**
fence	**bákod**
floor	**sahíg**
garage	**garáhe**
garden	**hardín; hálamanán**
gate	**tárangkahan**
ground space	**sílong**
(beneath house)	
gutter	**alulód**
house	**báhay**
kitchen	**kusína**
kitchen (2nd or maid's)	**dirty kitchen**
living room	**sala**
patio (covered or indoor)	**lanai**
post	**póste; halígi**
porch	**portico**
roof	**bubóng**
room	**kuwárto; silíd**
sink	**labábo**

staircase	**hagdánan**
stairs; steps	**hagdán**
storeroom	**bodéga**
terrace	**teres**
toilet	**kasílas**
upstairs	**itaás**
wall	**dingdíng**
window	**bintána**
window sill	**pasimáno**
water storage & wash area	**batalán**
yard	**bakúran**

Household Items
(Mga bagay sa sambahayan)

air conditioner	**air con**
bed	**káma**
bed spread	**kubrekáma**
bench; stool	**angkó**
blanket	**kúmot**
cabinet	**kábinet**
calendar	**kalendáryo**
carpet	**karpét**
chair	**sílya**
clock	**orasán**
closet	**aparadór**
cupboard	**paminggálan**
curtain	**kurtína**
divan	**pápag**
dresser	**tokadór**
fan (electric)	**bentiladór**
flower vase	**ploréra**
light; lamp	**ílaw**
mat	**baníg**
mattress	**kutsón**

mirror	**salamín**
mosquito net	**kulambó**
picture; photo	**retráto**
piano	**piyáno**
pillow	**únan**
pillow case	**pundá**
radio	**rádyo**
rocking chair	**silyón;**
	tumbatumba
rug	**alpombra**
sheet	**kúmot**
sofa; couch	**sopá**
stereo	**istéryo**
table	**mésa**
television	**telebisyón**
transistor radio	**transistór**
trunk	**baó**
wash tub	**batyá**

Kitchen Items
(Mga Bagay sa Kusina)

basin	**palanggána**
bowl	**mangkók**
broom	**walís**
can opener	**abreláta**
casserole	**kaseróla**
colander	**salaán**
cooking vat	**talyase**
dining table	**mésa; hapág kainán**
dipper	**tábo**
drinking glass	**báso**
faucet	**grípo**
frying pan	**kawáli**
jar (earthen) for:	
-water storage	**tapáyan**
-drinking water	**banga**

kettle	**kaldéro**
kitchen knife	**kutsilyo**
ladle	**sandók**
mortar (for rice)	**lusóng**
oven	**óben; pugón**
pail	**timbá; baldé**
pitcher	**pitsél**
platter	**bandehádo**
pot	**palayók**
pot cover	**takíp ng palayók**
pot ring stand	**dikín**
rag	**basáhan; trápo**
refrigerator	**frigidaire; repridyirédor**
shredder; grater	**kudkúran**
sink	**labábo; hugasán**
spatula	**siyansé**
stove	**kalán**
strainer; sifter	**salaán**
table cloth	**mantél; tapéte**
winnowing basket	**biláo**

TOOLS *(Mga kasangkapan)*

axe	**palakól**
hammer	**martílyo**
hoe	**asaró**
ladder	**hagdán**
nails	**páko**
plane	**katám**
pliers	**plaís**
plow	**aráro**
saw	**lagarì**
screw	**tornílyo**
screwdriver	**disturnilyadór**
shovel; spade	**pála**

sickle; scythe	**kárit**
wrench	**liyábe**

AUTO PARTS *(Mga bahaging kotse)*

air conditioner	**air con**
axle	**ehe**
back wheel	**gulóng sa hulihán**
battery	**bateryá**
bearing	**bering**
bolt	**perno**
brake	**preno**
carburetor	**karburetor**
clutch	**klats**
differential	**diperensiyál**
engine	**motór**
exhaust	**eksost**
fan	**bentiladór**
front wheel	**gulóng sa harapán**
gasoline	**gasolina**
generator	**dyeneretor**
grease	**grasa; mantika**
hood	**hud**
inner tube	**interyór**
key	**súsi**
lights	**mga ilaw**
light bulb	**bombilya**
mud guard	**tapalodo**
nut	**tuerka**
oil	**langis**
pump	**bomba**
radiator	**radyetor**
spark plug	**isparplag**
tank	**tanké**
tire	**goma; (gulóng)**
valve	**bálbula**

| wheel | gulóng; ruweda |
| windshield | bintána ng kótse |

PROFESSIONS & OCCUPATIONS
(Mgá Propesyón at Mgá Hanapbúhay)

actor/actress	artísta
architect	arkitékto
author/writer	mánunulat
ballerina	baylarína
barber	barbéro
bill collector	kubradór
businessperson	mángangalakál
butcher	mangangátay
carpenter	karpentéro(a)
cashier	kahéro(a)
clerk; typist	klerk; táypis
conductor (bus/train)	kunduktór(a)
cook	kusinéro(a)
dancer	mananáyaw
dentist	dentísta
doctor	doktór
driver (horse rig)	kutséro
driver (vehicle); chauffer	tsupér
electrician	elektrisísta
engineer	inhinyéro
employee	empleádo(a)
farmer	magsasaká
firefighter	bombéro
fisherperson	mangingisdá
foreperson	kapatás
fortune-teller	manhuhulâ
garbage collector	basuréro
gardener	hardinéero
hairdresser	mangungúlot
housewife/keeper	táong-báhay

ironing woman	**plantsadóra**
janitor	**diyánitor**
jewelry maker	**alahéro**
laborer	**piyón**
landlord/lady	**kaséro(a)**
landowner	**asindéro(a)**
laundrywoman	**labandéra**
lawyer	**abogádo**
maid/houseboy	**katúlong**
postal carrier	**kartéro**
manager	**mánidyer**
manicurist	**manikurísta**
mason	**kantéro**
mechanic	**mekániko**
messenger	**mensahéro**
midwife	**komadróna**
musician	**musikéro(a)**
nurse	**nars**
nursemaid; governess	**yáya**
optometrist	**optómetra**
painter *(artist, house, etc)*	**pintór**
pharmacist	**parmasiyútiko(a)**
photographer	**retratísta**
pianist	**piyanista**
pilot	**pilóto(a)**
plumber	**tubéro**
policeman	**pulís**
porter/longshoreman	**kargadór**
principal	**prinsipál**
sailor	**maríno**
sales clerk	**ahénte**
scientist	**siyentipiko**
sculptor/sculptress	**iskultór(a)**
seamstress	**modísta**
secretary	**sekretárya**
shoemaker	**sapatéro**

singer	**mágangantá**
soldier	**káwal; sundálo**
storekeeper/vendor	**tindéro(a)**
street cleaner	**kaminéro(a)**
student	**estudyánte**
tailor	**sastré**
teacher	**gúro; títser**
thief	**magnanákaw**
tenant (land only)	**kasamá**
ticket-seller (theater)	**takilyero(a)**
unemployed	**waláng trabáho**
waiter/waitress	**serbidór(a); wéyter/wéytres**
worker	**manggagawa**

NATIONALITIES
(Mga Iba't-ibang Lahi)

Arab	**Arábe**
Australian	**Ostralyáno**
Canadian	**Kanádyan**
Chinese	**Intsík, Insík**
African	**Aprikáno**
American	**Amerikáno(a)**
Dutch	**Holandés**
English	**Inglés**
French	**Pransés**
German	**Alemán**
Greek	**Griyégo**
Native American	**Indiyan**
Indian	**Bumbáy**
Indonesian	**Indunísyan**
Italian	**Italyáno**
Japanese	**Hapón**
Korean	**Koreáno**
Mexican	**Mehikáno**

Philippino	**Pilipino(a)**
Russian	**Rúso**
Spanish	**Kastíla**
Swiss	**Swíso**
Vietnamese	**Byetnamís**

GOVERNMENT OFFICIALS
(Mga Tagapamahala sa Gobiyerno)

President	**Presidénte**
Vice president	**Bise-Presidénte**
Secretary	**Sekretárya**
Senator	**Senadór**
Governor	**Gobernadór**
Vice govenor	**Bise-Gobernadór**
Representative	**Representánte**
Mayor	**Alkálde; Méyor**
Vice mayor	**Bise-Akálde**
Councilor	**Konsehál**
Treasurer	**Tresoréro**
Judge	**Hukóm; Huwés**
Police chief	**Hépe (ng Pulís)**
Barangay captain	**Kapitán del Barángay or Barrio**

Grammar Notes: Tagalog based nouns do not change to reflect gender. Many Spanish based nouns change endings to reflect gender. The letter "a" is added as the last letter of the noun to reflect the female gender. Where the noun ends in "o", male gender, it is replaced by "a" to indicate the female gender. The potential for gender switch is indicated in the text by an *"(a)"* following the noun.

*(e.g. waiter=serbidor; waitress=serbidóra
male pilot = piloto; female pilot = pilota)*

THE CHURCH *(Iglesya/Simbahan)*

Catholic Church...........	**Iglesya Katóliko -or-**
	Simbáhang Katóliko
Protestant Church.......	**Iglesya Protestante**
Baptist Church.............	**Iglesya Bautista**
Church of Christ..........	**Iglesya ni Cristo**
Episcopal Church.........	**Iglesya Episkopal**
Methodist Church........	**Iglesya Metodista**
Presbyterian Church.....	**Iglesya Presbiteryana**
Jewish Synagogue.......	**Sinagogang Hudyo**

Church Officials:

The Pope	**Ang Pápa**
Cardinal	**Kardinál**
Archbishop	**Arsobíspo**
Bishop	**Obíspo**
Priest	**Pári; Páre; Pádre**
Minister	**Minístro; Pastór**
Mother Superior	**Mádre Superiyóra**
Nun	**Mádre; Móngha**
Deacon	**Diyakáno; Dikáno**
Rector	**Rektór**
Missionary	**Misyenéro**

Vocabulary:

altar, shrine	**altár**
alterboy	**sakristán**
cathedral	**katedrál**
candle	**kandilá**
Christ	**Cristo**
chapel	**kapilya**
church	**iglesya; simbáhan**
church bells	**kampaná**

cross	**krús; kurús**
God	**Diyós/Bathalá**
Holy Virgin	**Mahál na Birhen**
kneel	**lumuhód**
mass	**mísa**
pray	**Dálangin**
prayer	**dasál**
sermon	**sérmon**

USEFUL PHRASES:

Let's go to church.
Tayó na sa simbáhan.

Let's go to mass.
Tayó na sa mísa.

Take me to the (Catholic Church).
Dalhín mo akó sa (Iglesia Katolika).

Take us to the (Baptist Church).
Dalhín mo kamí sa (Iglesia Bautista).

Is this the way to the (Church)?
Itó ba and daáng patúngo sa (Iglesia)?

Kneel and pray.
Lumuhód ka at magdasál.

CULTURAL NOTES: *The Philippines is the only Christian country in Asia. Over 80% of the population is Catholic. The Church influences almost every aspect of social and political life.*

DIRECTIONS *(mga dako)*

| to the left | | sa kaliwâ |
| to the right | | sa kánan |

left	kaliwâ	right	kánan
straight	dirétso	stop!	pára!
up	ibábaw	down	ibabâ
front	haráp	back	paurong
beside	tabí	past	lampás

	between	gitnâ
	across	ibáyo

north	hilága	south	tímog
east	silángan	west	kanlúran

MUSIC AND INSTRUMENTS
(tugtog at mga instrumento)

band	bánda
concert	konsiyerto
dance	sayáw
flute	pláuta
guitar	gitára
harmonica	silíndro
mandolin	mandolín
note	nóta
organ	órgano; órgan
performer	artísta
piano	piyáno
show	palabás
singer	mangangantá
song	kanta
violin	biyolín

GAMES AND ACTIVITIES
(Mga laro at mga gawain)

baseball	**beisból**
basketball	**basketból**
billiards	**bilyár**
cockfight	**sábong; tupáda**
fencing (with rattan staffs)	**arnis**
golf	**golp**
horse race	**karera**
ping-pong	**ping-pong**
tennis	**ténis**
volleyball	**báliból;*sipa**
jai alai*	**jai alaí**

*(a version of volleyball played with the feet)

Cultural Notes: Cockfighting is the most popular sport in the Philippines. Cockpits are found almost everywhere. The cockpits come to life on weekends and holidays. No program is ever drawn up. Betting is often conducted on the honor system with participants expected to remember the odds of their transaction. The fights are decided when one of the cocks, each of which has a double bladed spur attached to his claw, turns tail or is maimed to submission. The winning cock must confirm his superiority by pecking twice at the loser. If not, the fight is ruled a draw.

METALS *(mga bakal)*

copper	**tansó**
gold	**gintó**
iron	**bákal**
silver	**pílak**
steel	**asero**
tin	**estanyo**

FAUNA

Animals *(mga hayop)*

bat	**paníki**
bear	**soó**
bull	**tóro**
carabao (*water buffalo*)	**kalabáw**
cat; kitten	**púsa; kutíng**
clam	**halaán**
cow	**báka**
crocodile	**buwáya**
deer	**usá**
dog; puppy	**áso; tutá**
eel	**ígat**
elephant	**elepánte**
fish	**isdá**
frog	**palaká**
goat	**kambíng**
gecko	**butikí**
horse	**kabáyo**
lion	**león; liyón**
lizard (large)	**bayáwak**
leech	**lintá**
monkey	**unggóy; tsónggo**
mouse, rat	**dagá**
mule	**mulá**
pig	**báboy**
pig (suckling)	**kulíg**
pig (wild)	**báboy-ramó**
pig (young)	**biík**
rabbit	**kuného**
sheep	**túpa**
snake	**áhas**
tiger	**tígre**
turtle	**pagóng**
wolf	**lóbo**

Birds *(mga ibon)*

chick	**sísiw**
chicken	**manók**
crow	**uwák**
dove; pigeon	**kalapáti**
duck	**páto; bíbe**
eagle	**ágila**
goose	**gansá**
hawk	**láwin**
hen	**inahín**
kingfisher	**piskadór**
owl	**kuwágo**
parrot	**lóro**
quail	**púgo**
rooster	**tandáng**
turkey	**pábo**
wild chicken	**labúyo**

Insects *(mga kulisap)*

ant	**langgám**
bee	**bubúyog**
beetle	**salagúbang**
butterfly	**paruparó**
coconut beetle	**uwáng**
caterpillar	**hígad**
centipede	**alupíhan**
chicken flea	**hánip**
cockroach	**ípis**
dragonfly	**tutubí**
firefly	**alitaptáp**
flea	**pulgas**
fly	**lángaw; bángaw**

locust	**bálang**
lice (louse)	**kúto**
mosquito	**lamók**
moth	**gamu-gamó**
termite	**ánay**
scorpion	**alakdán**
spider	**gagambá**
wasp; hornet	**putaktí**
worm	**úod**

FLORA

abaca *(manila hemp)*	**abaká**
acacia tree *(monkey pod)*	**akásya**
bamboo	**kawáyan**
betel nut palm	**búnga**
bouganvilla	**bugambílya**
brunfelsia	**dáma de nóche**
	(Lady of the Night)
champak	**tsampáka**
coconut	**niyóg**
cotton	**búlak**
cotton tree	**kápok**
dahlia	**dálya**
gardenia	**rosál**
ginger; ginger lily	**kámya**
grass	**damó**
guava	**bayábas**
hibiscus	**gumaméla**
jasmin	**hasmín**
lily	**líryo**
Mexican creeper	**kadéna de amór**
	(Chain of Love)
mahogany	**kamagóng**
narra	**nára**

orchid	órkid; dápo
pakalana	ílang-ílang
plumeria	kalatsútsi
palm tree	anáhaw
rice plant	pálay
rattan	ratán
rose	rósas
sugar cane	tubó
tuberose	asuséna
yacca tree	yakál

Vocabulary:

bark	balát
branch; stem	sangá
bud	búko
flower	bulaklák
fruit	prútas; búnga
leaf	dáhon
plant	haláman; taním
root	ugát
seed	butó
tree	póno
tree trunk	púno
twig	siít

MOTHER NATURE

air; wind; breeze	hángin
bright, clear	maliwánag
calm	tahímik
cloud; fog; mist	úlap*
cold; chilly	malamíg
dark	madilím
dawn, sunrise	madalíng-áraw
dew	hamóg

drizzle; shower	**ambón**
dust	**alikabók***
earthquake; tremor	**lindól**
eclipse	**eklípse**
fire, flame	**apóy**
hot, warm	**maínit**
humid	**umído**
lightning	**kidlát**
moon	**buwán**
mud	**pútik***
rain	**ulán***
rainbow	**bahaghári**
rainy season	**tag-ulán**
sand	**buhángin***
sky, heavens	**lángit**
smoke	**asó; úsok***
soil	**lúpa**
star	**bituín**
stone	**bató**
sun	**áraw***
thunder	**kulóg**
thunderstorm	**unós**
twilight	**takipsílim**
typhoon; storm	**bagyó**
wave	**alon***
snow	**busílak**
volcanic ash	**lahár**
sunshine	**sínag-áraw**

Grammar Note:

* add prefix **ma-** to the indicated word to change it to an adjective:*(e.g. **ulap**=cloud; **maulap**=cloudy; **araw**=sun; **maaraw**=sunny)*

TOPOGRAPHICAL TERMS

bay; gulf	**loók**
beach	**apláya**
bridge	**tuláy**
cave	**kuwéba; yungíb**
coast	**baybáyin**
creek; stream	**sápa**
desert	**disyérto**
east	**silángan**
farm; rice field	**búkid**
forest; jungle	**gúbat**
hill	**buról**
hilltop	**gulód**
island	**ísla; puló**
lagoon	**baí**
lake	**láwa**
meadow	**párang**
mountain	**bundók**
mountain pass	**siláng; lagúsan**
north	**hilága**
ocean; sea	**dágat**
plain	**kapatágan**
port; wharf	**daúngan**
reef	**bahúra**
river	**ílog**
river mouth	**láwa**
road; street	**daán; kálye**
seashore	**baybáy**
south	**timog**
town	**báyan**
valley	**lambák; libís**
volcano	**bulkán**
waterfall	**talón**
west	**kanlúran**

THE BODY *(Ang katawan)*

abdomen	**pusón**
ankle	**bukung-bukúng**
arm	**bráso; bísig**
armpit	**kilikíli**
artery	**malakíng ugát**
back	**likód**
blood	**dugó**
body	**katawán**
bone	**butó**
brain	**útak**
breast	**súso**
brow	**noó**
buttocks	**puwít**
calf (of leg)	**kalamnán ng bintí**
cheek	**pisngí**
chest	**dibdíb**
chin	**bába**
clitoris	**tilín**
ear	**ténga; taínga**
elbow	**síko**
eyebrow	**kílay**
eye; eye-lash	**matá; pilikmatá**
face	**mukhá**
finger	**dalíri**
finger (little)	**kalingkíngan**
foot	**paá**
forehead	**noó**
gums	**gilagid**
hair	**buhók**
hair, body	**balahíbo**
hand	**kamáy**
head	**úlo**
heart	**púso**
heel	**sákong**

hip	**balakáng; pigí**
intestine	**bitúka**
intestine (large)	**ísaw**
jaw	**pangá**
kidney	**bató**
knee	**túhod**
leg (lower)	**bintí**
leg (upper)	**hitá**
lip (lower)	**lábi**
lip (upper)	**ngusò**
lung	**bága**
mouth	**bibíg**
nail	**kukó**
navel	**púsod**
neck	**leég**
nipple	**utóng**
nose	**ilóng**
palm	**pálad**
penis	**títi**
pubic hair	**bulból**
rectum	**tumbóng**
ribs	**tadyáng**
shin	**lulód**
shoulder	**balíkat**
skin	**balát**
sole (of foot)	**talampákan**
stomach	**tiyán**
testicle	**bayág**
thigh	**híta**
throat	**lalamúnan**
thumb	**hinlalakí**
toe	**dalíri ng paá**
tongue	**díla**
tooth	**ngípin**
tooth (molar)	**bagáng**

uterus	**baháy-batá**
vagina	**púki; kíki**
vein	**ugát**
wrist	**pulsó**

Vocabulary:

abcess	**magá**
bald	**kalbó; panót**
beard	**balbás**
birthmark; blemish	**pilat**
boil	**pigsá**
bowlegged	**sakáng**
castrated	**kapón**
chills; malaria	**ngíki**
circumcised	**tulí**
diarrhea	**diarea; kursó**
dimples	**biloy**
dysentary	**íti**
enema	**labatíba**
eyeglasses	**salamín**
fever	**lagnát**
false teeth	**pustíso**
freckles	**pékas**
gas pains	**kabag**
gray hair	**úban**
lap (of woman)	**kandúngan**
mole	**nunál**
nausea	**alibadbád**
pregnant	**buntís**
pyorrhea	**piyorea**
scab	**langíb**
scar	**péklat**
stye (in eye)	**kulíti**
swelling	**búkol**
tumor	**túmor**

ulcer	**úlcerá**
vaccination	**bakúna**
vomit	**súka**
wart	**kulugó**

USEFUL PHRASES

I have a sore or aching *(back, tooth, throat)*.
Masakít ang *(likod, ngipin, lalamúnan)* ko.
I have a fever.
Nilálagnat akó.

I vomited this morning.
Násuká akó kaninang umága.

I feel like vomiting.
Para akóng másusuká.

I have a cold.
Násipón akó.

I am very sick.
Masamáng-masamâ ang katawán ko.

I have gas pains.
May kabag akó.

Where can I find a doctor?
Saán may doktór?

Call a doctor!
Itawag mo akó ng doktór!

Send for a doctor!
Magpatawag ka ng doktór!

DESCRIPTIVE ADJECTIVES

absent-minded	**malilimutín**
active	**maliksí**
alive	**buháy**
angry	**galít**
bad	**masamâ**
bashful	**hiyâ**
beautiful	**magandá**
big	**malakí**
bitter	**mapaít**
bland	**matabáng**
boastful	**hambóg**
boisterous	**harót**
braggart	**mayábang**
brave	**matápang**
brightly colored	**matingkád**
broken	**sirà**
bruised	**bugbóg**
burned; burnt	**sunóg**
calm	**tahímik**
careful; cautious	**maíngat**
cheap	**múra**
cheerful	**masayá**
chewy	**makúnat**
circular	**bilóg**
clean	**malínis**
cloudy	**maúlap**
coarse	**magaspáng**
cold	**malamíg**
comical	**kómiko/a**
conceited	**mayábang**
cooked	**lutô**
couragous	**metápang**
courteous	**magálang**

coward	**duwág**
crazy	**lóko; lukú-lukó**
creased	**gusót**
crisp	**malutóng**
crooked	**baluktót**
crude	**magasláw**
cruel	**malupít**
dark *(complexioned)*	**maitím**
dark	**madilím**
dashing	**makísig**
dead	**patáy**
decayed	**bulók**
deep	**malálim**
delicate	**marupók**
delicious	**masaráp**
delightful	**nakatútuwâ**
destroyed	**sirà**
difficult	**masípag**
dirty	**marumí**
disorderly	**maguló**
drunk	**lasíng**
dull	**mapuról**
dumb	**bóbo**
durable	**matíbay**
dusty	**maalikabók**
early	**maága**
empty	**waláng lamán**
exhausted *(physically)*	**malatâ**
expensive	**mahál**
faded	**kupás**
fair *(complexioned)*	**maputì**
fast	**mabilís**
fat	**matabâ**
few	**ilán**
fickle	**pabágu-bágo**

fine *(OK)*	mabúti
fine *(smooth)*	píno; makínas
flabby *(body)*	malatâ
foolish	ulól
foul-smelling	mabahò
fragile	marupók
fragrant	mabangó
fresh	saríwa
full	punô
funny	nakakátawá
gentlemanly	maginoó
good	mabaít
good *(weather)*	magandá
gossipy; gossiper	tsismóso/a
handsome	guwápo
happy	maligáya
hard	matigás
heavy	mabigát
high	mataás
honest	matapát
hot	maínit
humble	mabábang-loób
humid	úmido
ignorant	ignoránte
industrious	masípag
inexpensive	múra
inside-out	baliktád; baligtád
insolent	bastós
intelligent	matalíno; marúnong
ironed	plantsádo
kind	mabaít
late	hulí
lazy	tamád
level; even	pátag
liar	sinungáling

light *(weight)*	**magaán**
light-colored	**maputlâ**
likeable	**nakatútuwâ**
long	**mahabà**
loose	**maluwág**
low	**mabába**
loyal	**matapát**
many	**marámi**
mature	**magúlang**
mischievous	**pílyo/a**
modest	**mahinhín**
muddy	**mapútik**
naked *(waist down)*	**hubó**
naked *(waist up)*	**hubád**
naked; nude	**hubú't-hubád**
narrow	**makítid**
naughty	**pílyo/a**
new	**bágo**
nice	**magandá**
noisy	**maíngay**
nutritious	**masustánsya**
oily	**malangís**
old *(things)*	**lumà**
old *(person)*	**matandâ**
old-fashioned	**makalúma**
pale	**maputlâ**
patient	**matiyagâ**
pitiful	**káwawà**
playboy/girl *(flirt)*	**palikéro/a**
plenty	**marámi**
polite	**magálang**
poor	**mahírap**
pressed	**plantsádo**
quiet	**tahímik**
rainy	**maulán**

rancid	**maantá**
raw	**hiláw**
rectangular	**rektánggulo**
refined	**mahinhín**
resilient	**makúnat**
restless	**malikót**
rich	**mayáman**
ripe	**hinóg**
rotten	**bulók**
rough	**magaspáng**
round	**bilóg**
rowdy	**magúlo**
rude	**bastós**
rugged; not level	**bakú-bakó**
sad	**malungkót**
salty	**maálat**
shallow	**mabábaw**
shameless	**waláng-hiyâ**
sharp	**matalím**
shiny	**makintáb**
short	**maiklî; maiksî**
short *(person)*	**pandák**
short tempered	**maiklî ang pagtitimpî**
shy	**mahiyáin**
sincere	**matapát**
slim *(person)*	**balangkinitan**
slow	**mabágal**
small	**maliít**
smooth *(flat)*	**makínis**
snobbish	**supládo/a**
snug	**masikíp**
soft	**malambót**
soggy *(food)*	**malatâ**
sour	**maásim**
spicy-hot	**maangháng**

spoiled *(fish)*	**bilasâ**
stout	**matabâ**
strict	**mabagsík**
strong	**malakás.**
stupid	**gagá o tangá**
sturdy	**matíbay**
stylish	**móda**
sweet	**matamís**
talkative	**daldál**
tall	**mataás; matangkád**
tasty	**malása**
tattletale	**tsismóso/a**
tender	**malambót**
thick	**makapál**
thin	**manipís**
thin *(person)*	**payát**
tight	**masikíp**
timid	**dungô**
tough	**matigás**
transparent	**naaanínag**
truthful	**matapát**
twisted	**balikukô**
ugly	**pángit**
unripe	**hiláw**
upside-down	**baligtád; baliktád**
vain	**banidóso/a**
warm	**maínit**
weak	**mahinà**
wet	**basâ**
wide	**malápad**
wilted	**lantá**
windy	**mahángin**
wise	**marúnong**
wrinkled; creased	**lukót**
young	**batà**

COMMANDS

Grammar notes: *use "ka" for "you" (singular);* **"kayo"** *for "you" (plural).*

Come!	**Pumaríto kayó!**
Come home!	**Umuwî ka!**
Count!	**Bumílang ka!**
Cry!	**Umiyák ka!**
Dance!	**Sumayáw kayó!**
Drink!	**Uminóm kayó!**
Eat!	**Kumáin kayó!**
Go along!	**Sumáma kayó!**
Go outside!	**Lumábas ka!**
Get lost!	**Alís diyán!**
Jump!	**Tumalón ka!**
Kneel!	**Lumuhód kayó!**
Laugh!	**Tumáwa kayó!**
Leave! Go away!	**Umalís ka!**
Read!	**Bumása ka!**
Run!	**Tumakbó ka!**
Shout!	**Sumigáw kayó!**
Sing!	**Kumantá kayó!**
Sit!	**Umupô kayó!**
Stand!	**Tumayô kayó!**
Swim!	**Lumangóy ka!**
Turn around!	**Umíkot kayó!**
Walk!	**Lumákad kayó!**
Write!	**Sumúlat ka!**

Negative Commands

Grammar Notes: To convert Commands to Negative Commands omit **"ka/kayo"** *and add* **"Huwag"** *and* **"kang"** *(singular) or* **"kayong"** *(plural) before the verb.*

Don't come!	**Huwag kayóng pumaríto!**
Don't come home!	**Huwag kang umuwî!**
Don't cry!	**Huwag kang umiyák!**
Don't eat!	**Huwag kayong kumáin!**
Don't leave!	**Huwag kang umalís!**
Don't shout!	**Huwag kang sumigáw!**

WEIGHTS & MEASURES

Vocabulary:

inch	**pulgáda**
foot	**talampákan; piyé**
yard	**yárda**
mile	**mílya**
ounce	**ónsa**
pound	**líbra**
square meter	**métro kuwadrádo**
centimeter	**sentimétro**
meter	**métro**
kilometer	**kilométro**
gram	**gramó**
hectogram	**guhít**
metric ton	**toneláda**
hectare	**ektárya**

Linear Measure:

12 inches	= 1 foot	=	0.3048 meter
3 feet	= 1 yard	=	0.9144 meter
100 cm	= 1 meter	=	1.0936 yard
1,000 meters	= 1 kilometer	=	0.6214 miles

Weight Measure:

100 grams	= 1 hectogram	=	3.5 ounces
10 hectograms	= 1 kilogram	=	2.2 pounds
100 kilograms	= 1 metric ton	=	1.1 U.S. ton

Land Measure:

43,560 sq. ft.	= 4,840 sq. yards	= 1 acre
1 hectare	= 10,000 sq mtr	= 2.471 acres

Liquid Measure:

1 liter	=	1.05 quarts	=	2.1 pints
1 gallon	=	4.00 quarts	=	3.785 liters

Temperature:

(Centigrade temperature is used in the Philippines)

To convert Centigrade (^oC) to Fahrenheit (^oF):

$$^oC = 5/9 \ (^oF - 32)$$

To convert Fahrenheit (^oF) to Centigrade (^oC):

$$^oF = 9/5 \ (^oC + 32)$$

0° F = -18^oC	32° F = 0^oC
50° F = 10^oC	60° F = 15.6^oC
70° F = 21.1^oC	80° F = 27^oC
90° F = 32.2^oC	98.6^o F = 37^oC
100^oF = 37.8^oC	105° F = 40.6^oC
110^oF = 43.3^oC	212° F = 100^oC

PILIPINO-ENGLISH

DICTIONARY

PILIPINO-ENGLISH

A

abá	exclamation of surprise
abúhan; astre	ashtray
adiyós	goodbye
áhas	snake
ahénte	agent
abó	ashes
agád	at once; soon
Agósto	August
akalà	idea, belief
ákín	mine, my
akó	I
aksidénte	accident
álaala	memory; gift
aláhas	jewelry
álat	salt
alikabók	dust
alín	which
alís	departure
álisan	to remove from
alisín	to remove
áliwan	entertainment, pastime
almusál	breakfast
álon	wave
amá	father
amerikána	man's coat
ámin	our, ours (excl. you)
amóy	smell, odor
anák	child
ang	the *(article: - singular)*

ang mgá	the *(article)*
áni	harvest
aníno	shadow
anó	what
antayin	to wait for
anunsiyo	announcement
anyáya	invitation
apóy	flame (of fire)
aráro	plow
áraw	day; sun
árte	art
asáwa	husband (or wife)
ásim	sour taste
asín	salt
asó	smoke
áso	dog
aspilé	pin
asúkal	sugar
asúl	blue
at	and
átin	our, ours (incl. you)
awá	pity *(n)*
áway	quarrel, fight
ay	*(particle:* equiv. of - to be)
áy	exclamation of dispair
áyos	order, arrangement
aywán	don't know

B

ba	*(part:* question marker ?)
babá	chin; lowness
babáe	female, woman
babalík	will be back

Brownout	electrical power outage
báboy	pig, pork
bága	lungs
bágal	slow; sluggish
bágo	new; before
bagyó	typhoon; storm
bahá	flood
bahági	a part, portion
bahála na!	"Come what may!"
báhay	house
baitáng	grade; step of staircase
baká	*(part: expresses doubt)*
báka	cow
bákal	iron, steel
bákit	why
bákod	fence
bakúran	yard
bakyâ	wooden shoes
bálak	plan, purpose, goal
balat	leather; skin; crust; cover
bálíkan	round trip
balità	news
bálot	wrapping
balútan	package
bandilà	flag, banner
bangkâ	boat
bangkó	bank
bansá	nation, country
bantáy	watchman, guard
bapór	ship, boat
barbéro	barber
barberyá	barbershop
baríl	gun, revolver

baság	broken
basag-ulo	quarrel, altercation
baso	drinking glass
bastón	walking stick; cane
batá	child
batás	law
batì	greeting
bató	stone; kidney
báwa't	every, each
báwal	forbidden, prohibited
báyad	payment
báyan	town; country
bayani	hero
bérde	green
bestído	dress
bibíg	mouth
bigás	rice
bigát	weight, heaviness
biglâ	suddenly, at once
bílang	number, numeral
bilanggô	prisoner
bilanggúan	prison
bilí	to buy; to purchase
bílin	to make a request
bintaná	window
binyág	baptism
birò	joke
bísig	arm, forearm
biyáhe	trip, travel
Biyérnes	Friday
bombílya	electric light bulb
bóses	voice

bóte	bottle
buhángin	sand
buháy	alive; growing
búhay	life
buhók	hair
bukás	open
búkas	tomorrow
búkid	field; farm
bukód (sa)	besides; in addition to
buksán	to open
bulaklák	flower
bulsá	pocket (pants or shirt)
bumalík	return
bumása	to read
bumilí	to buy
bundók	mountain
burdado	embroidered
bútil	grain; cereal
butó	bone; seed
butónes	buttons
buwán	moon; month
buwíg	bunch
buwís	tax
buwísit	bad luck

C

Note: The Pilipino equivalent of the letter "C" is the letter "K" - the third letter of the Pilipino alphabet. For simpilicity, English alphabetical order is maintained throughout this dictionary.

D

daán	road, street
daán	a unit of hundred
dakilà	great; foremost
dalhán	to bring someone something
dalhín	to bring something
dalî	quickness; promptness
damdámin	emotion; suffering
damít	cloth; dress
dangál	honor
dápat	must; ought
dáti	former; formerly
datíng	arrival; coming
daw	it is said
despidida	going away party
dibdíb	chest; breast
dilà	tongue
diláw	yellow
diligín	to water; sprinkle
dilím	dark; darkness
din	also; too
diperensyia	problem; difference
disgrásya	accident
díto (or **ríto**)	here, in this place
Disyémbre	December
diyán	there, in that place
diyáryo	newspaper
Diyós	God; Supreme Being
doktór	medical doctor
doón	there, over there
doséna	dozen
dugó	blood
dúlo	end; point

dumatíng	to arrive
dumi	dirt; refuse
dúnong	knowledge; wisdom
duwág	coward
dúyan	hammock; cradle

E

edád	age
edukádo	educated; trained
edukasyón	education
eksámen	examination; test
eléktrika	electric
eleksiyón	election; voting
elebétor	elevator
empáke	packing; wrapping
Enéro	January
entabládo	stage
eskuwéla	school
espesiyál	special; good
estasyón	station; waiting shed
estudiyánte	student
éto (or heto)	here; here it is

G

gáano	how much; how many
gabí	night; evening
gáling (sa)	comes from; came from
galít	angry
gálit	anger
gámit	use; usefulness
gamítin	to use

gamót	medicine
gamutín	to cure
gandá	beauty
ganitó	like this
ganyán	like that
gátas	milk
gawáng-kamáy	handmade
gáya	imitation
gayón din	same; also; likewise
ginisá	sautéed food
ginoó	gentleman; mister; sir
gintô	gold
gisíng	awake
gisíngin	to wake up someone
gitnâ	middle; center
góma	rubber; tires
grádo	grade; class
gripó	faucet
gúlang	age
gúlay	vegetable
gunting	scissors
gupít	haircut
gupitin	to cut with sissors
guró	teacher
gusalî	building
gustó	like; desire; want
gutóm	hungry
gútom	hunger

H

habà	length
habâ	elongated

hábang	while; as long as
hagdán	ladder; stairs
halagá	cost; importance
hálalan	election; voting
halík	kiss
halíka	come here
halimbawá	example
hámak	lowly; despised
handaán	celebration; party
hangál	ignorant; stupid
hanggáng	until
hángin	wind; air; atmosphere
hápon	afternoon
hapúnan	supper
haráp	front
hardin	garden
hardinero	gardener
harî	king
harína	flour
harót	unladylike; unrefined
hátinggabí	midnight
hátol	judgement; decision
háwak	hold
hawákan	to hold
háyop	animal
héto	here; here it is
hilagà	north
hindî	no; not
hiningá	breath
hinlalakí	thumb
hinóg	ripe
hiláw	unripe; raw
hintayín	to wait for
hípon	shrimp

hirám	borrowed
hiramín	to borrow
hiyâ	shame
ho (or **po**)	term(s) for respect
Hoy	Hi
húkbo	army
hulí	late; tardy
húlog	to fall; to drop
Húlyo	July
humigâ	to lie down
humingî	to request; to ask for
Húnyo	June
hustó	sufficient, adequate
huwág	don't, do not
Huwébes	Thursday
huwés	judge

I

ibá	other; another; different
ibabá	under; below; down
ibábaw	above; on
ibáyo	opposite; double
íbig	want; like; wish; desire
ibigáy	to give
íbon	bird
ikáw	you *(singular)*
ilagáy	to put; to place
ilálim	beneath
ilán	some; how many
ílaw	light fixture; lamp
ílog	river
ílong	nose
impúnto	exactly (referring to time)

iná	mother
íngay	noise
inggít	envy
ínit	heat; warmth
inumín	drink; to drink
inúbó	coughing
inyó	your, yours
ipakilala	to be introduced
isáma	to take along; include
isará	to close *(windows or doors)*
isaulì	to return *(a borrowed item)*
isdá	fish
ísip	thought; mind
isuót	to wear; to put on
itaás	above; to put up
itápon	to throw away
itím	black
itlóg	egg
itó	this; this one
ituró	to teach; to show
íwan	to leave behind
iyák	cry
iyakin	tearful
iyán	that (nearby)
íyo	your; by you
iyón	that

K

ka	you
kaarawán	birthday
kababáyan	countryman
kabáyo	horse
kabihasnán	civilization

kabisádo	memorized
kabuháyan	livelihood
kabutíhan	goodness; virtue
kagabí	last night
kagalít	enemy
kagatín	to bite
kahápon	yesterday
kahón	box
káhoy	wood; lumber
kaibígan	friend
kailán	when
kailángan	to need; necessary
káin	food; eat
kakilála	acquaintance
kalabaw	carabao
kalahatí	half; one half
kalákal	merchandise; goods
kalán	clay-stove
kaláwag	rust
kalayáan	independence; liberty
kalésa	cart *(horse drawn, 2 wheel)*
kaligayáhan	happiness; contentment
kalíhim	secretary
kaliwâ	left *(direction)*
kálye	road, street
kamag-ának	relative
kamátayan	death
kamátis	tomato
kamáy	hand
kambal	twins
kamí	we *(excl. of person spoken to)*
kamisadéntro	shirt *(long sleeve with collar)*
kamisatsína	shirt *(collarless)*
kamiséta	undershirt

kampaná	churchbells
kánan	right *(direction)*
kandilá	candle
kanilá	their; theirs
kánin	cooked rice
kanína	a while ago
kaníno	whose
kaniyá	his; her
kanlúran	west
kanluranín	western
kantá	song
kapatíd	brother or sister
kapé	coffee
kápitbahay	neighbor
karapatán	right
karáyom	needle
kargáda	baggage
karné	meat
kasáma	partner *(in business)*
kasápi	member
kaseróla	casserole
kasí	because
kasílyas	toilet
kásiya	fits; fitting
katás	fruit juice
katawán	body
katúlad	like; similar
katúlong	helper; servant
káunti	few, little
káwad	wire
káwal	soldier
kawáli	frying pan
kawaní	employee
kawawá	pity *(adj.)*

káwawà	pitiful
kawáyan	bamboo
kay	to *(with names of persons)*
kayá	so; and so; that's why
kayó	you *(pl.)*
káysa	than
kayumanggí	skin color of Filipinos
kéndi	candy
késo	cheese
kinatawán	representative
kláse	class
ko	my, mine; by me *(-post)*
kukó	fingernail
kulambó	mosquito net
kúlay	color
kulóg	thunder
kumáin	to eat
kúmot	blanket
kumpuní	to mend; to repair; to fix
kumúha	to get
kumustá	How are you?
kundíman	native love song
kung	if; when, as to
kunsúlta	consultation
kurso	diarrhea
kurtína	curtain
kúru-kuró	opinion
kusiná	kitchen
kutsára	spoon
kutséro	rig driver
kutsílyo	table or kitchen knife
kuwadrádo	square
kuwádro	picture frame
kuwéro; kátad	leather
kuwintás	necklace

L

labá; paglalabá	to wash (clothes)
lában	against
labás	outside
Labasan	exit
labí	lower lip
labís	surplus; excessive
lábo	unclear; vague
labóg	overcooked
lagáy	condition; state
lagdá	signature
lagí	always
lahát	all, everybody
lahí	nationality; race
lákad	walk
lakás	strength
lakí	size
lalagyán	container
laláki	man; male
lalamúnan	throat
lámang	only
lamápit	approach; to come near
lambát	fishing net
lambót	soft; tender
lamíg	coldness
lamók	mosquito
lámpara	lamp
lána	wool
lángaw	fly, housefly
langgám	ant
langís	oil
langóy	swim
lantá	wilted; withered
lántsa	launch; motorboat
lápis	pencil

laráwan	picture
larô	play; game
laruán	plaything; toy
lása	taste
lasíng	drunk; drunkard
lásingan	bar; drinking place
láson	poison
láta	tin can
láway	saliva
layà; láyaw	freedom
láyas	to go away; to run away
layó	distance
láyon	aim; purpose
libra	pound
líbre	free; gratis
libró	book
ligáya	happiness
ligò	bath
líhim	secret
likás	native of
likhâ	creation; product
lindól	earthquake
linggó	week
Linggó	Sunday
línis	cleanliness
linísin	to clean
lípon	group
listáhan	list
litráto	picture
litsón	roast pig
loób	interior
lumá	not new, used
lumákad	to walk
lumálaki	growing, getting bigger
lumangóy	to swim

lumipád	to fly
lumubóg	sink
Lúnes	Monday
lunsód	city
lupá	earth; ground; land
lutó	cooked
lutó	the cooking

M

maáarì	possible; can
maága	early
maálat	salty
maásim	sour
mababá	low
mabahò	putrid, rank
mabaít	good
mábanggâ	to bump; to collide
mabangó	fragrant
mabasâ	to become wet
mabigát	heavy
mabúhay	welcome; long live; to live
mabúti	good, well
madálang	slowly
madalás	often; frequent
madalí	easy; fast
madaling-áraw	dawn; sunrise
madilim	dark
madlâ	the public; all the people
mag-ának	family
mag-áral	to study
mag-asáwa	to marry; husband & wife
mag-ísip	to think
magálang	courteous
magalíng	good; excellent

magandá	beautiful; pretty
mágasín	magazine
magbilí	to sell
magbiyahe	to travel
magdasál	to pray *(Catholic)*
magháin	to set the table
maghápon	all day long
maghimatáy	to faint; lose consciousness
maghúgas	to wash (not clothes)
magkáno	How much?
magkapatíd	siblings
maglabá	to wash clothes
maglarô	to play
magpasyál	to take a walk
magsasaká	farmer
magsimbá	to hear mass / go to church
magtanim	to plant
mágulat	to be surprised
mahabà	long
mahál	dear; precious; expensive
mahírap poor	
mahusay	efficient; exceptional
maiklî	short
maíngay	noisy
mainggítin	envious
maínit	hot; warm
máintindihán	to understand
maís	corn
maitím	black
makabágo	modern, up-to-date
makabáyan	patriotic; nationalistic
makapál	thick
makatas	juicy
mákina	machine, sewing machine
makinárya	machinery

mákita	to see
makiúsap	to plead; to request
malakí	big, large
malamíg	cold; cool
malambót	soft
malapít	near
málay	knowledge; consciousness
malayà	free; independent
malayò	far; distant
malî	wrong; a mistake; error
maligáya	happy
maligò	to bathe
maliít	small
malínis	clean
maliwánag	clear, bright
malusóg	healthy
mamâ	mister
mámayâ	citizen
mamilì	choose
mamilí	to go shopping
manahî	to sew
manalángin	to pray *(Protestant)*
mánanahî	by and by; later on
mámamayan	seamstress
manlalaro	player
maniwalà	to believe
manók	chicken
mantikà	lard
mantikilya	butter
mapagbirô	jester; joker
mapaputí	white
marámi	much; many
marká	grade; trade mark
Márso	March
Martes	Tuesday

marumí	dirty
marúnong	intelligent; wise
masyado	utmost; more than enough
masamâ	bad; wicked
masaráp	delicious; pleasant
masayá	happy; cheerful
masípag	industrious
matá	eye
matáas	high
matabâ	fat
matagál	long (time)
matákot	to be afraid
matamís	sweet
matandâ	old; aged; an old person
matangkád	tall
matigás	hard
matuwâ	to be glad
maúhaw	to be thirsty
maulán	rainy
maútak	intelligent
may	(var. of mayroón) *(particle)*
may-arí	owner
maybáhay	wife
mayáman	rich, wealthy
Máyo	May
mayroón	to have / possess; there is
maysakít	patient; sick person
médiyas	socks; stockings
médyo-hiláw	medium-rare
médyo-lutò	medium-well
ménos	less; minus
merienda	snack; AM/PM snack break
mésa	table
minúto	minute
mísa	mass *(religious)*

míting	meeting
Miyérkoles	Wednesday
mgá	*(part.)* (pluralizes count nouns)
mo	your; by you *(sing.)* -post
mukhâ	face
mulâ sa	from
mulî	again
múra	cheap

N, Ng

na	already *(adv)*; that, who which (pron)
nagagalak	happy; glad; pleased
nakatirá	living in; resident of
namán	also, too
namatáy	died
námin	our; by us (exclusive)
nápaka	very; utmost (prefix)
naparíto	came
naparoón	went
nárito	here
nároon	there
nása	(particle expressing position, location, or direction)
násaán	where
nátin	our; we; us (incl)
nogósyo	business; industry
nérbiyos	nervousness; nerves
ngâ	(particle) please; really; truly
ngáwit	numbness
ngayón	now; today
ngíki	chills; malaria
ngípin	tooth
ngitî	smile

ngúni't	but
ngusò	upper lip
nguyâ	to chew
nilá	their, theirs
nínang	godmother
ninyó	your, yours
niyá	his, her
nínong	godfather
Nobyémbre	November
noó	forehead
noón	at that time
nóta	musical note
nunò	grandparent

O

o	or
obíspo	bishop
obligádo	obligated; forced
oditóryum	auditorium
oháles	buttonhole
ókra	okra
Oktubre	October
okupádo	occupied; busy
óo	yes
operasyón	operational; operation; operation (surgical)
opisína	office
opó, ohó	yes sir; yes ma'am
oportunidád	opportunity
óptiko	optician
oras	hour; time
orasán	clock
órbita	orbit
orihinál	original

orkéstra	orchestra
órkid	orchid
órder	(an) order; a serving (of food)
ordinaryo	ordinary; usual; common
órends	orange (color)
organisasyón	organization
organísmo	organism
O, síge	(expression) OK; all right
óso	bear
ospitál	hospital
otél	hotel
óyayi	lullaby

P

paá	foot
paalám	goodbye; farewell
paáno	how?
páaralán	school
pabuyá	tip; gratuity
padér	wall (concrete, brick or stone)
pagdatíng	arrival
páhayagan	newspaper
pag-ása	hope
pagkáin	food
pagód	tired; weary
pagsúlong	progress
pakí	please
pakinábang	profit, gain
pákò	nail
pakpák	wing
paksâ	subject; title; theme
pálad	fate; palm of hand
palagáy	opinion
palakpák	applause

palálò	proud; boastful
pálay	rice plant
pálayan	unhusked rice
paláyaw	nickname
paléngke	market
pámahalaan	government
pambansá	national
pamílya	family
panahón	season
panáog	to go down
pang-áhit	razor; shaver
pangakò	promise
pangálan	name
pangánib	danger
panginoón	master; lord
pángit	ugly
papél	paper
paraán	method; way
parého	same; similar
parmásya	pharmacy
paról	lantern
parúsa	punishment
pasinayà	inauguration
pasò	burnt flesh
pasô	pot for plants
patáy	dead; lifeless; extinguish
patnúgot	director; editor
páwis	perspiration
payák	simple
payát	thin
páyong	umbrella
Pebréro	February
péra	cent; centavo; money
péro	but

pílak	silver
pintá	paint
pintô	door
pípa	pipe
pirmí	always; permanent
pisngí	cheek
píso	peso
pistá	feast; birthday
pistang-bayan	town fiesta
plántsa	hot iron
platito	saucer
pláto	plate
plúma	fountain pen
po	(term for respect)
pósporo	match
prémyo	prize; reward
programa	program; plans
prutas	fruit
prútera	fruit tray
pugón	stove
pulá	red
pulbós	powder
pulído	polished; refined; polite
púlong	meeting
pulót-gatâ	honeymoon
pulpól	blunt; obtuse
pulúbi	beggar
punô	full
punó	leader; chief; tree
punong-lungsod	capital city
pusà	cat
pusò	heart
putî	white
putók	blast
puwéde	can; possible

R

rádyo	radio
raw (daw)	it is said
reklámo	complaint
relihiyón	religion
relós	watch
rikádo	condiments for cooking
riles	rails (train track)
ríto (or díto)	here
regálo	gift; present
réhas	grating; railing; bars
repáso	review
repinádo	refined
resérba	reserve
resérbado	reserved
resérbasyón	reservation
reséta	medical prescription
resíbo	receipt
rósas	1) rose plant; flowers
	2) pink color

S

sa	to; in; from; at; for; on
saán	where
Sábado	Saturday
sabáw	broth
sabáy	at the same time
sábi	what was said
sábihin	to tell
sabón	soap
saganà	abundant; plenty
ságing	bananas

sagót	answer
sáhod	salary; wage
saká	after that; then
sakâ	also
sakáy	passenger
sakím	selfish
sakit	sickness; pain
saksí	witness
sála	living room; sin
salámat	thanks
salamín	eyeglasses; looking glass
salapî	(collective) money; fifty centavos
salawál	trousers
saligáang-batás	constitution
salitâ	word; language
saló	to catch
sálu-sálo	party; banquet
sáma-sáma	altogether
samahán	to accompany
sambá	workmanship
sampû	ten
sandaán	one hundred
sandalî	a moment
sandók	ladle
sangá	branch
sapagká't	because
sapátos	shoes
sarádo	closed
sari-sarì	of various kinds
sariwà	fresh
sasakyán	vehicle of any kind
sayá	happy; cheerful
sáya	long skirt
sáyang	what a pity

sayáw	dance
séda	silk
sélyo	stamp (for letters)
sepilyo	a brush
séro	zero
servidór	server; waiter
sigarilyo	cigarettes
síge	let's go; go on; OK
sigurádo	sure; certain
sigúro	maybe; insurance
silángan	east; the Orient
silíd	room
silid-kainan	dining room
silid-tulugan	bedroom
sílya	chair
simbánan	church
siná	(plural of **si**)
síne	movie; cinema
sinélas	slippers
síno	who
sinúlid	thread
sípon	a cold (illness)
sirà	destruction
sirâ	broken; destroyed
siyudád (lunsod)	city
sóbre	envelope
sombréro	hat
sópas	soup
sorbétes	ice cream
sukà	vinegar
súkat	dirt; refuse
sukí	customer; patron
sukláy	comb
súlat	handwriting; letter (correspondence)

sumakáy	to ride in
sumáma	to go with
sumamba	to worship
sumunód	to follow
sundálo	soldier
súnog	fire
susí	key

T

taál	genuine
taás	height
tabâ	fat
tabák	sword; long bolo
tabáko	cigar; tobacco
tabíng-dágat	seashore
tablá	board; cut lumber
tag-áraw	summer; dry season
tag gutóm	famine
tag-ulán	rainy season
tagâ-saán	from where
tagumpáy	victory; triumph
tahî	sewing
taínga	ears
takíp	cover
takót	afraid
tákot	fear
taksil	traitor
talaán	list; record
talambúhay	biography
talì	a bundle; to tie
tamád	lazy
tanáwin	view, scenery
tangá	stupid; irresponsible

tanghalì	noon
tanggápan	office
taním	plant; tree
tanóng	question
tanyág	well-known; popular
táo	person; human being
taón	year
tapát	faithful; honest
tása	cup
táwa	laughter
táwad	bargain; reduction in price; pardon
tawíd	to cross; crossing
téla	cloth
tig	each
tíisin	sufferings
tiisín	to suffer; to be patient with
tíket	ticket
tíla	it seems
timbángan	scale; balance
tímog	south
tinapá	smoked fish
tindá	goods; anything for sale
tindáhan	store
tinidór	table-fork
tingnán	to look at; to see; to check
tínta	ink
totoó	true
trabájo	work; job
trayánggulo	triangular
trén	train
túbig	water
túhod	knee
tulâ	poem
tuláy	bridge

túlong	help; assistance
tungkól	about; referring to
tunóg	sound
tuntúnin	rule
tuwâ	gladness
tuwálya	towel
tuwíd	straight
tuyâ	sarcasm
tuyô	dry; dry fish

U

ubó	cough
úbod	coughing
úbod ng sípag	industrious
ugalì	custom; habit
ugát	blood vessel; root
úháw	thirst
úlan	rain; wet
úlap	cloud
ulî	once again
úling	charcoal
úlit	repetition; times (multiply)
úlo	head
umága	morning
umalís	to go away; to leave
umáwit	to sing
uminóm	to drink
umísip	to think
umpisá	beginning; the start
umupô	to sit
umuwî	to go home
úna	first
únan	pillow
úod	worm

úpa	pay; rent
upáng	so; so that
upisína	office
urí	kind; quality
úsapan	conversation
usapín	case in court
útak	brain
útang	debt
útos	command; order
uwí	anything brought home

W

wagás	sincere; genuine; pure
wakás	end
walâ	none; nothing; to be missing
waláng-hiyâ	shameless
waláng-págod	tireless
walís	broom
wastô	correct; right; in order
watáwat	flag; banner
wélga	strike (labor)
wikà	language

Y

'y médya	...and a half
yabág	footstep
yagbán	route
yago	sap; juice
yakag	invitation (by word of mouth)
yákap	embrace; hug

yakapin	to embrace
yáman	wealth; richness
yamót	annoyance
yangá	flowerpot
yangót	thick or heavy beard
yangyáng	hanging in the air to dry
yaníg	tremor (geological)
yantók	rattan
yapák	barefoot
yarì	made by; finished; done
yari	power; might; control
yedra	poison ivy
yelo	ice
yema	yolk of egg
yero	galvanized iron for roofing
yeso	chalk
yodo	iodine; type of disinfectant
yupî	dented
yutà	one hundred-thousand

ENGLISH-PILIPINO

DICTIONARY

ENGLISH-PILIPINO

A

a	isáng
about	tungkól sa
above	sa itaás; sa ibábaw
abundance	kasaganáan
abundant	saganà
accept	tanggapín
accompany	samáhan; saliwán
account	kuwénta
aching	sumasakít
act	gawâ
addition	dagdág
(to) add	dagdagán
adjustment	pag-aáyos
advertisement	anúnsiyo
after	pagkatápos
afternoon	hápon
again	mulî
against	lában sa
agreement	kasundúan
air	hangin
all	lahát
almost	hálos
already	na
also	din; rin
altar	altár; dambanà
although	káhi't
always	lagì; palagì
amount	halagá; kabuuán
amusement	libángan; áliwan
ancestor	ninunò

and	at
anger	gálit
angry	galít
animal	háyop
answer	sagót; tugón
approximately	bándang
April	Abríl
arch	arkó
area	láwak
argument	pagtatálo
arm	bráso; bísig
army	hukbó
(to) arrive	dumatíng
arrival	datíng
(will) arrive	darating
art	síning
as	gaya ng; túlad ng
ash	abó
ashtray	ábúhan; astre
ask	itanóng
asleep	tulóg
assist	tumúlong
assistant	katúlong
at	sa
ate	kumáin
attack	sumpóng (illness); paglúsob (war)
attend	dumaló
August	Agósto
authority	kapangyaríhan
avoid	iwásan
award	gantimpalà; pabuyà

B

baby	sanggól
bachelor	binatà
back	likód
(at the) back	sa likurán
by means of	sa manamagitan
buy	bumilí; bilhin
bad	masamâ
baggage	kargáda
balance	timbángan
ball	bóla
ballot	balóta
bamboo	kawáyan
banana	ságing
baptism	binyág
band	banda
barber	barbéro
bargain	táwad sa halagá
basin	palanggána
basket	básket; buslô
bath	paligò
bathe	maligò
bathroom	banyo; paliguán
beautiful	magandá
beauty	kagandáhan; gandá
because	sapagká't
become	maging
bed	káma
bedroom	silíd-tulugán
before	bágo; dáti
beggar	pulúbi
behavior	ugalì; gawî
belief	akalà
bell	kampanà; kampaníla
below	sa ibabá

belt	sinturón
beside	sa tabí
between	sa gitnâ
big	malakí
bird	íbon
bite	magatín
bitter	mapaít
black	itím; maitím
blanket	kúmot
blood	dugô
blow	hípan
blue	asúl; bugháw
boat	bangkâ; bapór
body	katawán
boiling	kumukulô
bone	butó
book	libró; aklát
borrow	humirám
boss	punô
bottle	bóte
bottom	ilálim
box	kahón
boy	bátang laláki
(house) boy	utusáng laláki
brain	útak
branch	sangá
bread	tinápay
breath	hiningá
bridge	tuláy
brief	maiklî
bright	maliwánag (luminous); marúunong (intelligent)
bring	dalhín
broken	sirâ; baság
broth	sabáw

brother	kapatíd na laláki
brother-in-law	bayáw
brown	kulay-tsokolate
brown (skin)	kayumanggí
brush	sepílyo
building	gusalì
bulb	bombílya
bullet	bála
bunch	buwíg
bundle	talí
burn	pasò
(to) burn	masúnog
burst	putók
business	negósyo
but	péro
butter	mantekilya
butterfly	paruparó
button	butónes

C

cake	keik; mamón
call	táwag
(to) call	tumáwag
care	alagà
(to) care	alagáan
careful	maíngat
carpenter	karpintéro
carry	dalhín
cat	pusà
cause	dahilán
celebrate	magdíwang
celebration	pagdiríwang; pistá
ceiling	kísame
center	gitnâ

chair	sílya; úpuan
chance	pagkakátaon
change	suklî (money); palít (exchange; substitute)
(to) change	palitán (exchange; convert)
cheap	múra
cheerful	masayá; masiglá
cheese	késo
chest	dibdíb
chicken	manók
chief	punò
child	batà; anák
chin	babà
choose	mamilí
Christmas	Paskó
church	iglesia; simbáhan
city	lunsód
(capital) city	púnong-lunsód
civilization	kabihasnán
class	kláse; urí
classroom	silíd-aralán
clean	malínis
clear	mal"inaw; maliwánag
climb	umakyát; akyatín
clock	reló; orasán
close	isará
clothing	damít
cloud	úlap
coal	karbón; úling
coat	amerikána
cold	malamíg
collar	kuwélyo
color	kúlay
comb	sukláy
come	pumaríto

comfort	alíw
(to) comfort	aliwín
committee	lúpon
companion	kasáma
condition	kalágayan; áyos
confidence	tiwalá
cook	kusinéro
(to) cook	maglutò
copy	kòpya
(to) copy	kópyahín
cork	tápon
corner	kánto
cost	halagá
cotton	búlak
cough	ubó
courage	tápang
courageous	matápang
courtesy	paggálang
cousin	pínsan
cover	takíp; takpán
cow	báka
coward	duwág
credit	útang
cross	kurús
cruel	malupít
cry	iyák
(to) cry	umiyák
cup	tása; kópa
curtain	kurtína
custom	ugalí
customer	sukí; tagabilí
cut	hiwá

D

damage	sirà
danger	pangánib
dangerous	mapangánib
dark	madilím
darkness	karimlán
daughter	anák na babáe
day	áraw
dead	patáy
dear	mahál
death	kamátayan
debt	útang
December	Disyémbre
deep	malálim
delicate	masélang
delicious	masaráp
departure	alís
describe	ilaráwan
description	paglalaráwan
dialect	wikaín
diaper	lampín
digestion	pantúnaw
diligent	masípag
direction	bandá
director	patnúgot
dirty	marumí
disaster	sakunâ
discussion	pagtatálo; pag-uúsap
disease	sakit
distance	layò; agwát
distant	malayò
divide	hatíin
dizzy	mahilo
(to) do	gawín

dog	áso
doll	manikà
door	pintúan
doubt	álinlangan
down	sa ibabâ
dozen	doséna
drama	dulâ
dress	barò; bestído
drink	inumín
(to) drink	uminóm
driver (of car)	tsupér
driver (of rig)	kutséro
(to) drop	mahúlog
(to) drown	malúnod
drunk	lasíng; langô
dry	tuyô
dumb (mute)	pípi
dumb (stupid)	hangál
dust	alikabók

E

ear	táynga
early	maága
earning	suweldo
earth	mundó; lupà
east	silángan
eastern	silangán
easy	madalî
eat	kumain; kain; kainin; kanin
education	pag-aáral
egg	itlóg
elbow	síko
election	eleksiyón; halálan;
electric	eléktrika

embarrass	hiyaín
embarrassed	nápahiyâ
employee	kawáni
end	wakás; katapusán
enough	sapát; hustó
entrance	pasukan
equal	magkapáris; magkatumbás
eraser	pamburá
error	pamburá
even	káhi't
even if	káhi"t na
evening	gabí
event	pangyayári
every	báwa't isá
everyone	lahát
exact	hustó; tamà
exactly	impúnto (referring to time)
example	halimbawà
exchange	magpalít; ipagpalít
expensive	mahál
experience	karanasán
eyebrow	kílay
eyelash	pilikmatá
eye	matá
eyes	mga matá
exit	labasan

F

face	mukhâ
(to) face	harapín
(to) fall	mahúlog
false	hindî totoó; dí-tapát
family	pamílya; mag-ának
far	malayò

fare	pasáhe; báyad
farm	búkid; kabukirán
farmer	magsasaká
fast	mabilís; matúlin
fat	matabâ
fate	kapaláran
father	amá
father-in-law	biyénang laláki
faucet	gripo
fault	kasalánan; malî
fear	tákot; pangambá
feather	balahíbo
February	Pebréro
feeble	mahinà
feeling	damdámin
feet	paá
female	babáe
fence	bákod
festivity	pistá; kasayáhan
fever	lagnát
few	kauntî; ilán
fight	áway; kágalitán; básag-ulo
fine	mabúti
finger	dalirì
fire	apóy; súnog
first	úna
fish	isdá
fix	ayúsin
flag	bandilà; watáwat
flame	níngas; apóy
flower	bulaklák
fly (insect)	lángaw
(to) fly	lumipád
follow	sumunód
food	pagkáin

for	para sa; para kay
force	lakás
forehead	noó
fork	tinidór
fragrance	bangó
fragrant	magbangó
free	malayà
freedom	kalayáan
frequent	madalás
fresh	sariwà
Friday	Biyérnes
friend	kaibígan
from	sa; búhat sa; mulâ sa
from where	taga saán
front	sa haráp
fruit	prútas
fry	ipiríto
full	punô
future	hináharáp

G

gain	tubò
game	larô
garage	garáhe
garden	hardín
garbage	basúra
general	henerál
get	kúnin
girl	bátang babáe
(to) give	bigyán; magbigáy; ibigáy
glass	báso; salamín
(to) go	pumaroón; pumuntá
goat	kambíng
godfather	nínong

godmother	nínang
gold	gintô
good	mabúti; mahúsay; maagalíng
government	pámahaláan
grain	bútil
grass	damó
grave	libíngan
great	dakilà
green	bérde; luntían
gray	grís; kúlay abó
group	lípon; pangkát
ground	giniling
ground beef	giniling na báka
guard	bantáy
(to) guard	bantayán
(to) guide	akáyin
gun	baríl

H

hair	buhók
half	kalahatì
hammer	martílyo; pamukpók
hand	kamáy
handmade	gawáng-kamáy
happy	masayá; maligáya
happy to	nagagalak
hard (difficult)	mahírap
hard (tough)	matigás
harvest	áni
hat	sambalíto
hate (anger)	matindíng gálit
have/has	may; mayroón
head	úlò; punò

headache	sakít ng úlo
health	kalusugán
healthy	malusóg
heart	pusò
heat	ínit
Hello!	Halo! (telephone greeting)
help	túlong
helper	katúlong
here	díto
hero	bayáni
Hi!	Hoy!
high	mataás
his/hers	niyá
history	kasaysáyan
hole	bútas
hope	pag-ása
horse	kabáyo
hospital	ospitál
hot	maínit
hour	óras
house	báhay; táhanan
houseboy	utusáng laláki
how	paáno
humble	mabábang-loób
husband	asáwa

I

I	akó
ice	yélo
ice cream	sorbétes; surbétes
idea	akalà
if	kung
important	mahalagá

in	sa; sa loób
indeed; really	ngâ
industrious	masípag
ink	tinta
inquire	magtanóng
insect	maliít na háyop; kulisáp
inside	sa loób
instrument	kasangkápan
insurance	segúro
intention	bálak; hangárin
introduced	ipakila
introduction	pagpagakilala
(to) invite	anyayáhan
iron	bákal
island	pulô
itchy	makatí

J

January	Enéro
jail	bilanggúan; piítan
jaw	pangá
jealousy	panibughô
jeepney	diyíp; diyípni
jewel	aláhas
join	pagsamáhin; pagdugtungín
joke	bíro
(to) joke	birúin
journey	paglalakbáy
judge	hukóm; huwés
juice	katás
July	Húlyo
June	Húnyo
(to) jump	tumalón; lumuksó

K

keep	itagò
key	susì
kick	sipáin
kind (type/class)	urì
kind (nice)	mabaít; maawaín
king	harí
kiss	halik
knee	túhod
kneel	lumuhód
knife	kutsílyo
knot	buhól
(to) know	málaman
knowledge	karunúngan; kaalamán

L

laborer	manggagawâ
ladle	sandók
lamp	lámpara
land	lupà
language	wikà
large	malakí
last	hulí sa lahát
late	hulí
later	mamayâ
(to) laugh	tumáwa
law	batás
lawyer	abugádo
lazy	tamád
lead	tinggâ
leader	punò

leaf	dáhon
learning	nag-áaral
leather	balát; kátad; kuwéro
(to) leave	umalís
(will) leave	aalís
(direction) left	kaliwâ
leg	bintî
less; minus	ménos
letter (corresp.)	súlat; líham
letter (alphabet)	títik
level	pátag; pantáy
liar	sinungáling
library	aklátan
lift	buhátin
light; lamp	ílaw
light (bright)	liwánag
light (weight)	magaán
(to) like	gustó; íbig
like (similar)	katúlad
line	gúhit
lip	labí
list	listáhan; talaán
listen	makiníg
(to) live (reside)	nakatirá
lock	kandádo
long	mahabà
look	tignán
loose	maluwág
loss	pagkawalâ
loud	malakás
love	pag-íbig
low	mababà
lumber	tablá; káhoy
lung	bagà

M

machine	mákina
mad	balíw
made	yarì
make	gawín
male	laláki
man	laláki
many	marámi
manager	tagápamahalà
map	mápa
March	Márso
market	paléngke
marriage	kasál
mat	baníg
match	pósporo
May	Máyo
maybe	segúro
meal	pagkáin
measure	súkat
meat	karné
medicine	gamót
medium	midyum
medium-rare	médyo-hiláw
medium-well	médyo-lutô
meeting	púlong; míting
memorize	isaúlo; kabisáhin
middle	gitnâ
milk	gátas
mind	ísip
mine	ákin
minute	minúto; sandalî
mixed	halu-halò
money	salapî
monkey	unggóy

month; moon	buwán
monument	bantayóg
more	mas
morning	umága
mosquito	lamók
mother	iná; nánay
mother-in-law	biyénang babáe
motorboat	lántsa
mountain	bundók
mouth	bibig
move	kumílos; gumaláw
much	marámi
music	tugtóg; tugtúgin
my; mine	ákin

N

nail; spike	pakò
naked	hubád (waist up); hubo (waist down); hubad-hubo (nude)
name	pangálan
narrow	makítid
nation	bansá; báyan
nature	kalikasán
near	malápit
necessary	kailángan
neck	leég
need	kailángan
needle	karáyom
neighbor	kápitbahay
new	bágo
news	balitá
nickname	paláyaw
night	gabí

no	hindî
noise	ingay
none	walâ
noon	tanghalì
north	hilagà
nose	ilóng
note	nóta
November	Nobyémbre
now	ngayón
number	bílang

O

obedient	masunúrin
October	Oktúbre
of	ng (nang)
offer	alukín
office	opisína
Oh!	O!
oil	langís
OK	síge; okey; tamà
old (people)	matandâ
old (things)	lumá
on	sa (ibábaw)
only	lámang
open	bukás
(to) open	buksán
opinion	kuru-kurò; palagáy
opposite	kasalungát
orange	dalandán
order (command)	útos
order (cleanliness)	áyos
organization	samahán; kapisánan
ornament	gayák; palamutí
other	ibá

our/ours	átin; námin' ámin; nátin
out	sa labás
oven	pugón
over	sa ibábaw
overtake	abutín
owner	may-arì

P

package	balutan
page	páhina; dáhon
pain	sakít
paint	pintúra
paper	papél
pardon	patáwad
parent	magúlang
past	nakaraán
paste	pandikít
(to) paste	idikit
payment	báyad
peace	katahimíkan
pen	plúma
pencil	lápis
perhaps	maráhil; sigúro
person; people	táo
pet	alágang-háyop
picture	laráwan
picture frame	kuwádro
pig	báboy
pin	aspilé
pity	awà
pitiful	kaáwaawà
plant	taním
plate	pláto; pinggán
pleased to	nagagalak

pleasure	kasiyáhang-loób
plow	aráro
pocket	bulsa
poison	láson
poor	mahírap
popular	bantóg; kilalá
post	póste; halígi
pot (for plants)	pasô
pot (for cooking)	palayok
potato	patátas
powder	pulbós
power	kapangyaríhan
(to) pray	magdasál (Catholic)
(to) pray	manalángin (Protestant)
present (gift)	handóg
present (time)	ngayón; kasalukúyan
price	halagá
prison	bilíbid; bilanggúan
process	paraán
proof	katibáyan
property	arí; ari-arìan
protest	lumában; sumalungát
public	pambáyan
pull	hiláhin; batákin
punishment	parúsa
purpose	bálak; láyon
push	itúlak
put	ilagáy

Q

quality	urì; klase
(good) quality	mabúting klase
quantity	dámi
quarrel	áway; kágalitán

queen	réyna
question	tanóng
quick	madalî
quiet	tahímik; waláng-kibô
quite	tíla
quiz	pagsúbok; pagsusúlit

R

railway	ríles
rain	ulán
rat	dagâ
raw	hiláw
rattan	yantók
razor	labáha
(to) read	bumása
ready	handá
reason	dahilán katwíran
receipt	resíbo
receive	tanggapín
record	talaán
red	pulá
religion	relihiyón
remember	alalahánin
remove	alisín
request	hilíng; kahilíngan
respect	paggálang
(to) respect	igálang
rest	pahingá
(to) rest	magpahingá
restroom	CR; Comfort Room
reward	gantimpalá
rhythm	kumpás
rice	bigás
rice (cooked)	kanin

rich	mayáman
right	tamá; wastô
right (direction)	kánan
ripe	hinóg
river	ílog
road	kálye; daán
roasted	iníhaw
roof	bubungán
room	silíd
root	ugát
rope	lúbid
rough	magaspáng
round	bilóg
round trip	balikan
(to) run	tumakbó
rust	kaláwang

S

sad	malungkót
safe	ligtás
salad	insaláda
salt	asin
salty	maálat
same	páris; parého; túlad
sand	buhángin
saucer	platíto
scale	timbángan
school	iskuwéla; páaralán
science	siyénsiya; aghám
sea	dágat
seat	sílya; úpuan
season	panahón
second	ikalawà; pangalawá
secret	líhim

secretary	sekretárya; kalíhim
see	mákita; tignán
seed	butó; binhî
send	ipadalá
sentence	pangungúsap
separate	hiwaláy
(to) separate	maghiwaláy
servant	katúlong; alilà
shallow	mabábaw
sharp	matálas; matúlis
shame	hiyâ; kahihiyán
shameless	waláng-hiyâ
sheep	túpa
ship	bapór
shirt	kamisadéntro; baró
shoes	sapátos
short	maiklî
side	tabí; tagilíran
signature	pirmá; lagdá
silk	séda
silver	pílak
sin	kasalánan
sister	kapatíd na babáe
size	lakí; súkat
skin	balát
skirt	saya; pálda
sky	lángit
sleep	matúlog
slow	mabágal; mahinà
slowly	madálang
small	maliít
smile	ngití
smoke	úsok
smooth	madulás
snake	áhas

sneeze	magbahíng
snore	hilík
(to) snore	maghilík
soap	sabón
socks	médyas
soft	malambót
some	ilán
son	anak na laláki
song	kantá; áwit
sour	maásim
sound	íngay; tunóg
soul	káluluwá
soup	sópas; sabáw
south	tímog
special	tangì
spoon	kutsára
spouse	asáwa
square	kudrádo; parisukát
staircase	hagdánan
stamp (letter)	selyo
star	bituín; talà
starch	almiról
station	istasyón
steam	singáw
step	hakbáng
sticky	malagkít
stiff	matigás
stingy	marámot
stomach	tiyán
stone	bató
story	kuwénto
stove	kalán; pugón
straight	deretso
street	kálye; daán
strength	lakás

strong	malakás
study	mag-áral
sudden	biglâ; kaagád
sugar	asúkal
summertag-	aráw
sun	áraw
Sunday	Linggó
supper	hapúnan
surname	apelyído; pang-angkán
sweet	matamís
swim	lumangóy
system	paraán

T

table	mésa; hápag
tail	buntót
tailor	sástre
take	kúnin
talk	magsalitâ
tall	mataás; matangkád
taste	lása; panlása
(to) taste	lasáhin; tikmán
tax	buwís
teaching	pagtuturò
teacher	gurò; maéstra
tear	luhà
teaspoon	kutsaríta
tell	sabíhin
than	kaysá
that	iyán; iyón
that's why	kayâ
there	doón; diyán
these	ang mga itó
thick	makapál

thief	magnanákaw
thin	payát
thing	bágay
this	itó
though	kahi't na
thought	ísip
thread	sinúlid
throat	lalamúnan
thumb	hinlalakí
thunder	kulóg
ticket	tíket
tight	masikíp
till	hanggáng
time	panahón; óras; sandalí
tin	láta
tired	pagód
to	sa
today	ngayón
toe	hinlalakí ng paá
together	magkasáma
toilet	kasílyas
tomorrow	búkas
tongue	dilà
too/also	din; rin; náman
tooth	ngípin
top	takíp
touch	hipò
town	báyan
trade	kálakalán
train	trén
tray	bandéha
travel	paglalakbáy
(to) travel	maglakbáy
treasurer	íngat-yáman
tree	punò

trousers	salawál
true	totoó
(to) turn left	kumaliwâ
(to) turn right	kumanan
twice	makálawá
twin	kambál
typhoon	bagyó

U

ugly	pángit
umbrella	páyong
under	sa ilálim
understand	máintindihán
up	sa itaás
upright	tuwíd
us	táyo; sa átin
use	gamítin
useful	mahalagá
utmost; very	napaka (prefix)

V

vacation	bakasyón
value	halagá
vegetable	gúlay
vehicle	sasakyán
verse	tulâ
very	masyádo
victory	tagumpáy
view	tánawin
vinegar	sukà
visit	dálaw
(to) visit	dumalaw

voice	bóses; tínig
vote	bóto
(to) vote	ibóto; ihalál
voyage	paglalakbáy

W

wage	sáhod
wait	maghintáy
waiting room	hintayan
walk	lumákad
walking stick	bastón
wall	dingdíng
war	giyéra
warm	maínit
wash	hugásan; maghúgas
wash (face)	paghíhilamos
wash (hands)	paghihináw
wash (clothes)	paglalabá; labá
wash basin/tub	hugasán
waste	dumí; basúra
watch (clock)	reló
watch (guard)	bantayán
water	túbig
wave	álon
we	kamí; táyo
weak	mahinà
weather	panahón
Wednesday	Miyérkoles
week	linggó
weight	bigát
well (water)	balón
well (fine)	mabúti
well done	lutung-lutô

HIPPOCRENE HANDY DICTIONARIES